Stuart Cable

Stuart Cable

From Cwmaman to the Stereophonics and Beyond

Jeff Collins

University of Wales Press Cardiff 2009

www.uwp.co.uk

British Library Cataloguing-in-Publication Data
A catalogue record for this book is available from the British Library.

ISBN 978-0-7083-2179-9
e-ISBN 978-0-7083-2283-3

Printed in Wales by Dinefwr Press, Llandybïe

CONTENTS

FOREWORD

I'm happy to be involved with this book about Stuart Cable. Although I live in America, I used to run into the Stereophonics every now and again. They were always eating hamburgers on the Sunset Strip in Hollywood when they'd be playing out here. Always burgers in some diner on the Strip! The first time I met Stuart, though, was at a charity event organized by Jimmy Page. That was a great night with so many wonderful musicians present. It brought out my inner fan! I felt more like a rock fan than a rock star, which was a nice feeling. And then I just joined in the giddy fun with the Stereophonics lads. We wanted to jam onstage. To do a song together. The guys asked me if we could all play one of The Cult's songs. Stuart wanted us to play 'Wildflower' from our *Electric* album. Now, singing is not my bag, so we had to write out the lyrics for Kelly. Nobody could think of the lyrics, though, so Stuart and me went to the bar and wrote out the words on napkins as we ran the music through our heads. It can be an enlightening experience doing that with rock lyrics!

I thought Stuart was a lion of a man. I've met Tom Jones a few times and Stuart has that same large, southern Welsh presence. He made me think of my favourite film of all time: *Zulu*. That movie shows how a small number of Welsh soldiers repelled an overwhelming number of Zulu warriors. It's the greatest film ever made in my opinion – on so many levels – we could write a book about why that film is genius. However, Stuart was like that whole Welsh regiment kind of thing. If I have to assess his character, I'd say he came across like that. I thought he was a stand-up and reliable guy – the kind you'd want in the trenches with you.

And I loved the Stereophonics. They were unashamed to rock. I felt they were a kindred spirit to The Cult. They had a similar musical upbringing to us. We came up at a time when everyone was afraid to be a rock band because of punk and we were the ones who put our heads above the parapet. In the same way, the Stereophonics came up in that post-grunge – you can't rock – era. But they made it also. It was a dream band from a village in Wales. It's very poetic.

Billy Duffy
Guitarist, The Cult

ACKNOWLEDGEMENTS

First, I have to thank Stuart Cable for being so generous with his time, patience and stories. He allowed me and my friend Andrew Pritchard (who took most of the photographs in this book) fantastic access to his new band – both backstage and in the studio. I find his story a fascinating one and hope you enjoy it as much.

Also, many thanks to Killing For Company: Greg Jones, Andy and Steve Williams and Richie King for putting up with my presence and questions at so many events.

Special thanks also to Jo Hunt for her amazing help and suggestions, particularly at the start of this project, and for making me feel so welcome at Monnow Valley Studio during my visits.

From the University of Wales Press, thanks to Ashley Drake for his suggestions and fine tuning, which helped this project develop. Thanks also to Sarah Lewis and Ennis Akpinar, for their constant help and support, and to Victoria Nickerson, Bethan James and Sarah Philpott.

Thanks as well go to Cathryn Scott for allowing me to use a quote from her interview with Kelly Jones about Stuart's departure from the band.

Extra special thanks go to Andrew Pritchard for all the photographs and the – unofficial – proofreading. Andrew's pointers and suggestions kept me on track.

Special thanks also to Yvonne for her invaluable support and help, without which this book would never have been finished – and to Bryn, for being Bryn.

Thanks also to Mum and Gordon for their help, and to my Dad for getting me interested in music in the first place.

INTRODUCTION

Stuart Cable: From Cwmaman to the Stereophonics and Beyond is a journey.

It's not a biography of Stuart Cable. It's not a detailed history of the Stereophonics. It's a tale that follows the journey made by a young drummer from a small, obscure village in Wales. It discovers how he rose to fame with a band, which would become one of the biggest groups in Europe.

On this journey, we find out how the Stereophonics got together, looking at their influences and how they created their music. This book examines how they battled their way to the top against all the odds! It also watches the dream fall apart as rifts develop in the band at the height of its fame, rifts that, ultimately, see Stuart leave the Stereophonics.

Finally we catch up with Stuart as he continues his journey with his new band, Killing For Company.

I hope you enjoy the trip!

I

PROLOGUE

You know what to get me for Christmas now. A beard. Wicked . . . I want a
big Dusty Hill ZZ Top one.

Stuart Cable, The Point, Cardiff, May 2007

It's a surprisingly cold evening for the end of May. It's 6 p.m. as I walk into
The Point in Cardiff: a church converted into a music venue in the city's
Bay area. Former Stereophonics drummer Stuart Cable is playing here
tonight with a new band, Killing For Company, which he has been carefully
assembling over the past year or so.

The first person I bump into is the band's affable manager, Jo Hunt.
She's handing the guest list over to the venue's owner. He does a double
take when he sees it. 'The band's list is limited to 30,' he says. 'Weren't you
told?' 'No,' says Jo, looking surprised. The guest list for Killing For
Company tops 70! 'It's all Stuart's fault,' she explains with a smile. 'He has
dozens of buses coming down from Cwmaman.'

Cwmaman is the former mining village in south Wales that is the
birthplace of both Stuart Cable and the Stereophonics. Stuart's already
been to the top of the rock tree as part of the Welsh three piece. They
topped the singles charts across Europe with songs like 'Traffic', 'The Bartender and the Thief' and 'Have a Nice Day'. The Stereophonics have sold
in excess of seven million albums, enjoying widespread success with albums
such as *Performance and Cocktails* and *Just Enough Education to Perform*.

Now Stuart Cable is attempting to climb back to the top with a new
band. It should prove an interesting journey for the larger-than-life drummer.
Although fired from the Stereophonics in acrimonious circumstances in
September 2003, Stuart Cable will not easily disappear into the back-
ground. He was the joker of the band, hugely entertaining with a big
personality and even bigger hair! He was easily the most recognizable
and, arguably, the most liked member of the band by fans and the press.

With me tonight is my friend and colleague Andrew Pritchard, who's
here to take photographs of this evening's performance: the first headline

gig by Killing For Company. We head upstairs to the dressing room, where any nerves are disguised by the band's pre-show banter. Stuart is in mid-discussion with lead singer Greg Jones about the dressing room's air-conditioning unit, which is standing two feet high off the ground with blinking red lights and futuristic space age buttons. Greg asks Stuart, 'What's R2-D2 doing here?' As he gets up from his chair, the drummer replies, 'Yeah. That's freaky! We don't need any Star Wars cast-offs in here.'

Stuart comes across to greet us and tells Andrew and me how excited he is about tonight's concert, not to mention the fact that the band has a prestigious support slot with The Who at Swansea's Liberty Stadium in just five days' time. We're introduced, one by one, to the band: Greg on vocals, bass player Steve Williams, rhythm guitarist Richie King and lead guitarist Andy Williams. Once the introductions are done, the banter resumes.

This evening there's a running joke about 1980s rock band Winger, famed for hits such as 'Seventeen' and 'Headed for a Heartbreak'. 'Can anyone name the drummer from Winger?' asks Simon Collier, who used to be Kelly Jones's guitar tech with the Stereophonics, but now works for the new band. His question is greeted by blank looks all around. 'Rob Morgenstein,' he reveals to groans across the room, as if it should have been startlingly obvious. 'No way,' shouts Steve Williams. 'You just made that up!' After this, for the rest of the evening, whenever anyone asks a question – any question! – the reply is always either Rob Morgenstein or Winger. This never fails to get a laugh. Never!

Andrew now asks the band if they'd mind posing for a few shots.

'Rob Morgenstein,' shouts Greg in reply.

'Do you want us all together, or just sitting casually?' asks Stuart, ignoring his lead singer's frivolity.

'Together,' Andrew tells them, also ignoring the running Winger gag. So they get ready to leave the dressing room and go up a set of stairs, just outside the room, which lead up to a landing and a stained glass window. 'What's my hair like?' asks Stuart to no one in particular. The famously curly-haired drummer looks into a mirror. 'Damn, I look like Rod Hull,' he moans in reference to the 1970s entertainer famous for his aggressive Emu puppet.

'You think that's bad?' asks Steve Williams. 'A little kid outside thought I looked like Jesus! This seven-year-old boy was walking past the venue, saw our poster and asked his dad if I was Jesus.'

'Fuck off! No way,' laughs Stuart at the tall bassist with his shoulder-length hair and biker's beard. 'I'd look like that as well if I could grow a beard,' continues Stuart with a big smile. 'It took me a week just to grow this little bit of stubble. I've always wanted to have a beard. You know what to get me for Christmas now. A beard. Wicked.'

'A white one with a Santa hat,' chips in their manager Jo, who has just entered the room.

'No!' says Stuart. 'I want a big Dusty Hill ZZ Top one.'

Once the photo shoot is over, the band returns to the dressing room one by one. Singer Greg, dressed in a black T-shirt with black jeans, heads straight for the fridge and grabs a bottle of water. The two guitarists enter together, arms around each other's shoulders. Andy, as lead guitarist, cuts a dash in true rock 'n' roll style. He's wearing a white vest, revealing colourful tattoos down his arms, a number of beaded necklaces, black jeans and cowboy boots. Richie, in contrast, is more subdued in a plain black T-shirt, three-quarterlength combat trousers, trainers and a blue beanie hat. He's the quietest member of the band.

As the guitarists take a handful of beers from the fridge and hand them to Stuart, Andrew and me, another of the road crew, Steve 'Hoppy' Hopkins, relates a tale from his time on the road in America with the Stereophonics. This one is about the time a state trooper pulled a gun on him in Fargo.

We were driving through the town, when suddenly a police car with a siren the size of a bucket appears right behind us. So I pull over. I thought I was going to jail. I was only on a holiday visa. I had no work permit, yet here I was touring with, and working for, the Stereophonics. I got out of the car. The trooper asked to see my driver's licence which I had tucked away in my front trouser pocket. The cop pulled out his gun. Now I was so scared that I dropped my wallet in the snow. Then the trooper made me lie face down in the snow – still pointing a gun at me! I decided not to say I was from Abercynon! I thought I was going down and was going to spend the next few years locked in a small cell with a big bloke called Bubba.

Everyone laughs. Steve Williams sits up quickly as he nearly spills his beer with laughter. Fortunately Hoppy avoided the hospitality of the local state jail and was able to continue his work on the tour.

The laughter slowly subsides. The band is very relaxed (at least on the outside) sitting on a sofa and chairs, which are arranged in a semi- circle at the far end of the dressing room.

Stuart's mobile phone rings. Its ringtone sounds remarkably like the chime of an ice-cream van.

'Anybody want a cone or a lolly?' quips Andy Williams.

'Ice cream. I want an ice cream,' shouts Stuart, mimicking the voice of a young child. It's an annoying voice. Then the drummer breaks into mock tears as he pretends he's dropped his ice cream on the floor. 'It is like that as a child, though, isn't it? When you see that van, you just go like this: ICEEE CREEAAMMM!' This time he shouts even louder in a child-like voice and pretends to be chasing after the van.

'No wonder you had to chase that van,' laughs Steve. 'You'd have scared them off looking like that! Imagine this curly haired kid running down the street, at full speed, screaming after the van. It's no wonder they sped off!' Everyone laughs at the image. 'My God. Imagine this crazy kid chasing them demanding sprinkles!' adds Andy, feeling sorry for the ice-cream van driver.

'Yeah!' agrees Stuart proudly. 'They're scared of this kid with all this fuzzy hair and I'm shouting at them "Come back and fight me!"'

By now Stuart's audience also includes three members of one of tonight's support bands: The Last Republic's singer and guitarist, John Owen, drummer Aron Harris and guitarist Dafydd Anthony are all sampling the hospitality backstage at The Point. For their first headline gig, Stuart's new band has decided to put on a strong show. The Last Republic is an impressive group destined for bigger things, given the right breaks. Upon entering the hall tonight, singer John handed me a copy of their EP recorded at the legendary Monnow Valley Studios in Monmouth, which the likes of Black Sabbath, Hawkwind and Robert Plant have all called home while recording. The Last Republic laid down four tracks there with producer Chris Sheldon, who's worked with the Foo Fighters, Radiohead and Roger Waters to name but a few. They've just come off stage playing what has been one of their biggest gigs so far. The band is still buzzing from the experience and enjoying being in the company of tonight's headliners. Another local band, Circle of One, is currently on stage in the hall below us. The crowd is lapping up their anthemic rock tracks like 'Automatic' and 'State of Grace', taken from their latest EP, *The Loud Minority*.

Killing For Company is not one of these bands who pick support acts on the basis that they won't be upstaged. Quite the opposite in fact. Guitarist Andy says it's important to get good support acts. 'Better to have them warming up the audience, so the crowd are really up for it when we come on and not bored stiff.' It's a refreshing point of view.

The band have selected and thoroughly rehearsed tonight's setlist. The running order is:

'She Won't Wait'
'The Boy Who Saw Everything'
'For The Taking'
'Secret Lives of Empty Bottles'
'Even After All'
'Reasons'
'Over'
'Conversation'
'Say About Me'
'Enemies'.

Time is now ticking. It's not long until the main act takes to the stage.

Stuart asks their manager Jo, 'Are they strict with the times here? Because we have our set timed at around 50 minutes. Shall we take a song out? We've got 10 songs and we're planning to do the download single "Enemies" last.'

'No,' says Jo. 'You've got an hour, so don't drop anything.'

Jo Hunt is the wise head guiding the band in these early days. Jo has worked for the V2 record label, where she worked closely with Stuart and the Stereophonics, and she also owns Monnow Valley Studios.

'Great,' replies Stuart. 'So we'll still play the 10 songs. Excellent.'

Backstage it's decided that, as this is the band's first headline gig, someone should introduce them on stage. 'Jeff has radio experience,' says Jo with a smile. 'I'm sure he'll happily do it for you.' So with minutes left, I'm duly nominated. My friend Andrew gives me a pat on the back and cheerily quips 'Don't mess it up' as he walks out of the dressing room toward the main hall to get ready to photograph the band in action.

The band follow him but head out to the backstage area singing a parody of a Kiss song to hide any nerves. 'God gave sausage rolls to you, gave sausage rolls to you . . .' they sing in unison. Stuart in particular warms to the theme. We pause outside a black curtain hiding the stairs which lead to The Point's stage. The venue can hold around 500 people.

It's time! Leaving the band anxiously waiting to get started, I slowly walk up onto the dark stage with just a single spotlight for illumination. I've heard a handful of tracks by this new band and I'm looking forward to finally seeing them live. Backstage, Stuart's determination to take this group to the top has been clear. He's carefully assembled a very talented band. It's obvious that he knows what he wants and how to get it. Most importantly he's done it once before. As I cross the stage, I think about how the Stereophonics first rose out of an unheard of village in south Wales to become one of Europe's top bands, selling millions of albums. No one – except close friends and family – had given them a chance of making it. Yet, against all the odds, the Stereophonics turned themselves into a major attraction. I make a mental note to find out more about Stuart's rise to success as I grab hold of the microphone and introduce the band to the eagerly awaiting audience.

Welcome to The Point. We've had two great acts, but this is the moment we've all been waiting for. On Friday they're playing Swansea's Liberty Stadium with The Who. Tonight they're here at The Point. Let's rock. It's Killing For Company.

2

CWMAMAN – THE BEGINNING

It's like when Lynyrd Skynyrd used to call their rehearsal room 'The Hell-hole'. They used to sleep there. We never slept here, but it was a hellhole!
Stuart Cable, Cwmaman, June 2007

I'm driving up the A470, one of the main roads from the Welsh capital, Cardiff to the valleys of south Wales. Andrew Pritchard is sitting in the passenger seat and we have the Stereophonics's debut LP *Word Gets Around* blasting out on the car stereo. Andrew and I are travelling to meet the group's former drummer Stuart Cable at his, and the Stereophonics's, home village of Cwmaman. The name is Welsh for 'Aman valley', after the river Aman which flows through the village. Before the arrival of the Stereophonics, it's fair to say 99.9 per cent of people had never heard of the place, which lies near the Welsh town of Aberdare. As with many communities in the south Wales valleys, Cwmaman was developed to house and provide services for workers in the local mines. The opening of the collieries in the mid-nineteenth century led to a dramatic growth in both the population and number of buildings within the village.

Coal was the very reason – the sole reason – for Cwmaman's existence. Its growth was, therefore, linked to the development of the coal industry. But the pits, which first opened in 1848, were gone more than one hundred years later. In the 1990s, the village boasted a population of less than four thousand people. Yet, in 1996 it came to the attention of music lovers worldwide when Richard Branson signed the Stereophonics as the first band for his newly formed V2 label.

This is the destination to which Andrew and I are heading. Two days ago, we watched as the former Stereophonics drummer performed his first headline gig with his new band, Killing For Company. It was a big success. Andrew and I saw the band for the first time – as did the most of the 500-strong crowd at The Point in Cardiff. The songs were slightly heavier in vibe than those of Stuart's former band, but still retained that anthemic, sing-along quality. After the gig, Stuart Cable told us,

I thought it went really well actually! There were one or two technical things that went a bit wrong early on. My monitor wasn't working properly for the first few songs. It was diabolical. But we just got on with the show. The problem resolved itself eventually and, on the whole, as a gig, I thought it was fantastic. There's a great balance to the band. We wrote these songs together and, I think, we write well as a group. I think our songs have the same impact as the first two Stereophonics albums. In fact, I feel this band's songs are very similar in quality to the early Stereophonics stuff.

It means I've got lots of confidence in this band – the same kind of confidence I had back then in the Stereophonics! When we first started doing support slots back in the 90s, we knew we could win the crowd over and it's the same now with this band. Greg Jones is a very charismatic lead singer. Andy Williams is a natural lead guitarist, while Steve Williams is awesome on the bass. Then you have Richie King, who's a different kind of guitar player. He's like AC/DC's Malcolm Young. He's that essential second guitarist. You take his guitar line away and you really miss it. Plus we've got great songs to back it up. We've got all the elements there.

Stuart's confidence is not misplaced. His new band has the talent, the potential and the songs to go a long way. But you also need 'the big break', a mixture of being in the right place, at the right time, plus careful and intelligent management.

The band's potential has really excited both Andrew and me. So we're looking forward to visiting the birthplace of Stuart's first break-through band. We're almost at Cwmaman. Once through the town of Aberdare, we follow the signs through the twisting streets of the village of Abercwmboi, until we arrive in Cwmaman itself. We're meeting Stuart at the community centre where he and the Stereophonics first rehearsed in their fledgling incarnation as Zephyr. We drive through Brynmair Road, along Fforchaman Road, past the Cwmaman Institute and then turn a sharp right into Mountain Road for a few yards before turning left into Glanaman Road and then passing a small building.

'That's the place,' points Andrew. 'Look! That's got to be the community centre.'

I slow down and look across the passenger seat from the steering wheel. 'No way!' I exclaim. 'That's far too small. There's no way the band rehearsed there. You couldn't fit a gang of anorexic mice in there!'

I stop the car soon after as the street becomes a dead end. This is the end of the line.

'Damn! We must have missed it!' I say, pointing out the startlingly obvious to my equally mystified passenger. We turn around and head back down to the Cwmaman Institute and park up by the nearby post office. I stop the car, get out and call Stuart on my mobile phone.

'Hi. We're here in Cwmaman, but we must have missed the community centre!'

He laughs. Then I'm given directions and get back into the car.

'It's back where we came from. I think. Well, according to what Stuart says,' I tell Andrew. So we head back down the road and seconds later we see the man himself. Stuart's standing right in front of the same building that I had dismissed as too small.

'See!' says Andrew. 'That's the place. I knew it was!' He beams a smug smile of satisfaction, which I decide – quite rightly in my view – to ignore.

We park up across the road and get out to meet Mr Cable. Behind us is a row of narrow terraced houses, while in front of us, past the community centre, fields stretch up to a vast array of mountains and forestry. It's a beautiful view.

'Alright, Jeff!' He shakes my hand with a firm grip, a huge smile and a gentle laugh. 'How are you, Andy? Welcome to Cwmaman: the birth-place of the Stereophonics!' Stuart pauses and looks around at his home village. His mother's house is just a few hundred yards away, back down the road. He still knows pretty much everyone here.

This is Cwmaman community centre. It's right here at the top of the village, where you can't go any further. As you can see, the bus stop is here. The buses have to turn around, because they can't go any further. There's no through road in Cwmaman. And if you go to that mountain over there (he points away from Cwmaman), you go into Mardy and the Rhondda Valley. So there's no passing traffic here. It means everyone knows everyone else. That's why people will now be out on the street wondering what we're doing! And they'll probably say 'Oh look. It's only Stuart Cable talking about the Stereophonics again.' So, yeah, this is where we used to rehearse. We kept all our gear here as well. It's like when Lynyrd Skynyrd used to call their rehearsal room 'The Hellhole'. They used to sleep there. We never slept here, but it was a hellhole! I don't know whether we can go in? Let's go around the corner here and take a look through the window.

The centre is locked, but Stuart leads Andrew and me around to the back of the small building for a peek inside. Stuart gets up onto tiptoes, grabs the window frame and peers inside.

Yep! We rehearsed here – my word – since day one really. We started in Kelly's father's garage, which is about 500 yards down the road. And then, when we had some more members join the band, we came here. We're talking years before our eventual bassist Richard Jones joined. You're probably talking five, or six, years before Richard came on board! We were a five-piece band at first, and this place had been built about five years previous to that. I remember asking the lady across the road, Shirley Evans, if we could we rehearse here. I explained that we were a band and she said 'Fine. I don't think anyone will object.' And that's what we used to do. We'd come here and religiously spend every Thursday and Sunday in here, rehearsing. All of the songs from the first album were written in this room [he says with obvious pride]! You know it's mad coming back here. Look, they've got some nice blinds up! It used to be terrible red curtains in our day.

Stuart steps down and shakes his head in disgust at the memory of those foul-coloured curtains.

I ask Stuart how he first met Kelly Jones and set the ball rolling for what would become the Stereophonics.

'My word!' he says pausing to remember. 'Jeez. Me and Kelly go back a really long way, because we lived just seven doors away from each other in the same street. His parents and my mother still live in the same houses just down the road there.' Stuart points at the homes just a few hundred yards down the road from where we are standing.

We all knew each other. There was a real sense of community, because, like I said, there's no passing traffic and no passing trade. So, really, I've known Kelly since he was old enough to walk and talk, because I was four years older than him. But in Cwmaman, there was always that kind of thing where everyone would bother with everybody. The young kids would hang out with the older kids. It didn't matter if there was a ten-year age gap. Didn't matter at all. The pool in Cwmaman also had a big part to play as well as it was a favourite place to congregate in the six weeks of school summer holidays.

Stuart once again peeks into the community centre as he recalls the first time he and Kelly hooked up, musically, in the mid-1980s.

The earliest memory – or the first thing that happened between Kelly and I – was when he was about ten. He had a guitar and started taking guitar lessons. Then I remember when he was about twelve, he knocked on my door. I had a drum kit. I'd managed to swindle £50 off my brother to buy this drum kit. I don't know why.

He laughs as he reflects back.

I had this silly idea that drums would be easy to play. God, was I wrong! When he first knocked on my door, Kelly had been rehearsing AC/DC's *Highway to Hell* album in his bedroom, while I was playing songs from the same album in my bedroom a few doors down. And he could hear me and I could hear him! So he just came up to the front door and said 'Do you fancy coming down to my old man's garage for a jam?' And that's how it started. Me and him. Just the two of us. Pretty bloody White Stripes really. Him playing guitar and me on drums.

We stroll a little way from the band's old rehearsal room. Stuart gazes down the road into the heart of the village. Then he breaks away from his private thoughts to resume the tale about the very beginning of what would become the Stereophonics.

When we really started playing, our first band was called Zephyr. They were mostly Kelly's age. It was Chris Davies on keyboards, Paul Rosser playing bass and a guy called Nicolas Geek on guitar. We would do the normal run-of-the-mill covers for the day. For example, Van Halen. We used to play 'Panama'! We did a bit of AC/DC as well, of course.

He smiles now as he harks back to those youthful attempts to play classic rock songs, some straightforward, others far more complex.
'And Rush. We used to attempt to play Rush,' he recalls with a smile. The Canadian hard rock band are renowned for their complex rhythms and chord structures.

Boy, we did Rush very, very badly. And, of all the Rush songs to try to play, we attempted their eleven-minute epic 'Xanadu'. I stand here now and think 'Why the hell couldn't we have tried something simpler, and shorter, like "Closer to the Heart"?' It would have been a lot bloody easier.

He smiles again at the naivety of youth. We walk back around to the front of the building as a bus passes us, slows down and parks up at the main stop just thirty yards from us.
'So that went on and we rehearsed, and rehearsed, and eventually we did our first gig.' Stuart pauses again and points to the corner of the road just across from where we are standing.

We did the gig there! But the club, which is standing there, is a different one now, because the first one burnt down. But we did our first gig there. It was April 7 1987! I'll never forget that date, because I can still see the posters on the lamp posts. I put them there! It was the Double Decker club and it was very different back then. And what you have to realize – and I'm sorry to go off on a bit of a tangent – but you have to realise that club land in Wales was huge in the 60s, 70s and 80s. It was where Tom Jones came through. It was huge in the north of England as well, where places like Batley Variety Club in Leeds would hold 3,000 people on a Saturday night. Well, we had a similar thing here, but on a smaller scale. Like that room up there would hold 275 people. We thought we'd put on a gig there. We were the first local band to do it and we thought we'd get about twenty people turn up. But when the night came, you couldn't move in there. The place was rammed to the rafters. I can always remember we opened up by playing 'Bad Moon Rising' by Creedance Clearwater Revival and then went straight into 'Hotel Califonia' by The Eagles. It probably sounded bloody atrocious! But everyone shouted and whistled like mad. They loved it! And then, well, you know what it's like once you go on stage – you kind of have the bug. You're hooked. So that was the first band: Kelly, Paul Rosser, Nicolas Geek, Chris Davies and myself as Zephyr. And it kind of went on for a couple of years. We started to write a couple of our own songs. They weren't great. [Stuart pauses.] Actually, they were bloody terrible.

As Andrew starts taking photographs of me interviewing Stuart, and of the community centre and the streets around it, the drummer tells me that eventually the time came for Zephyr to part company.

The band broke up. I started doing stuff with Nicolas Geek, while Kelly kept playing with Chris Davies and Paul Rosser. They started another band called Silent Runner, in which Kelly's cousin Gene played drums. And I started some other band, but basically they were both just mediocre pub cover bands playing blues rock.

It would be another two years before Stuart Cable and Kelly Jones hooked up again and got back on track, a route that would ultimately head away from the day-to-day grind of life in a small village to international music superstardom.

1. The joker in the pack! Stuart Cable was probably the most recognizable member of the Stereophonics. Copyright: Andrew Pritchard.

2. Cwmaman, 2007 – Stuart Cable with Jeff Collins outside the community centre in the village where the Stereophonics wrote and rehearsed their first two albums. Copyright: Andrew Pritchard.

3. Andrew Pritchard photographs Stuart Cable outside his birthplace in Cwmaman. Copyright: Jeff Collins.

4. The Stereophonic original line-up. From left to right: Stuart Cable (drums), Kelly Jones (guitars and vocals) and Richard Jones (bass). Copyright: Media Wales Ltd.

5. Roger Daltrey. Both the Stereophonics and Killing for Company played their first major gigs supporting The Who. Copyright: Andrew Pritchard.

6. Killing time! The clock ticks down as Stuart's new band Killing for Company wait to get precious rehearsal time ahead of their big gig with The Who. Copyright: Andrew Pritchard.

7. Souncheck. The roadies help Stuart set up his kit.

8. Showtime. Stuart leads his band onto the stage to support The Who at Swansea's Liberty Stadium.

9. Killing for Company on stage. Copyright: Andrew Pritchard.

10. On the drums – Stuart in action! Copyright: Andrew Pritchard.

11. Double life: Stuart carved out a successful career as a radio and TV broadcaster – seen here on XFM Wales in 2008. Copyright: Jeff Collins.

12. Killing For Company. Copyright: Andrew Pritchard.

13. Stuart in smoke. Copyright: Andrew Pritchard.

3

I NAME THIS BAND STEREOPHONICS!

Can I ask you one thing? Can you change your name? The one you have is terrible! Tragic Love Company! It's awful . . . You've got five days to come up with a new name, because that's when I'm printing the posters for the gig!
Promoter Wayne Coleman, 1995

Standing in the street where he grew up, Stuart Cable reflects on the next stage in his remarkable rise to the top of the music tree. Stuart is deep in thought, staring at the small community centre, where the Stereophonics used to write and rehearse. My friend Andrew is thirty yards away still taking photographs of Stuart's visit to Cwmaman with us. I'm just a few paces away.

'This was built to serve the community, by staging events such as coffee mornings, youth clubs and we also used to have birthday parties here. I had one! And Kelly had one.' Stuart breaks off when he notices me and Andrew giving him strange looks. He twigs what we are thinking. 'No!' he exclaims. 'When we were little, not when we were eighteen.' He bursts out laughing. 'Come on! Be serious, lads!' He steps closer to the centre.

I don't know if you can see in? (I step up to the window alongside Stuart and peer in through the glass.) If you look in there now, see that back wall over there? Well, I would sit there with my drums. We would play facing out towards the main door over there. So Kelly would stand on this side here, with Richard standing over there on the far side. It was the same way that we would always line up on stage. And that's also how we'd rehearse. In those early days, it was more about the rehearsal side of things. We'd got our repertoire of cover versions that we could go out and play live to earn £150 to £200 to pay the bills. When we were older, around twenty-two or twenty-three, it became all about writing songs here. I remember Kelly bought some four track recorder. So I've a lot of good memories from this place, really.

The first incarnation of the fledgling Stereophonics, Zephyr, had come to a slow end during 1989. Stuart and childhood friend Kelly

Jones had musically drifted apart. They were now playing in separate bands, both heading nowhere.

That went on for about two years. Then the two bands just kind of fizzled out. The place where me and Kelly got back together was one of these great landmarks of Cwmaman which have, over the years, disappeared. It was the pub that we used to drink in called the Ivy Bush. It's such a shame now because it's gone. I think that's sacrilege! Someone has bought it and turned it into a private house. Our local pub has become their home! It's not right. I remember being in there one Saturday night in 1991. Kelly was there and he came over to me to ask what I was doing. I said, 'Nothing.' So he asked if I fancied joining him for a jam. At this stage, I was twenty-one and Kelly was seventeen. I told him that I would join him for a session, but on one condition: I told him 'I'm not doing any of this pub rock blues shit. I wanna write some songs of our own.'

Fortunately for Stuart, Kelly was on the same wavelength.

It was great. Kelly told me that he wanted the same thing: to do less covers and write original material. So great! We both came back up here, to this very hall, to rehearse. And we had this guy, who was a bass player in one of Kelly's old bands, called Mark Everett. He was playing with us when we'd reunited. But we did a bit of a bad thing to him really. He went on holiday for two weeks. But me and Kelly were eager to get on with the band and start writing stuff. So Kelly said 'I know this guy Richard, who plays bass. You know, Richard Jones? He hasn't been playing long, but he's a decent bass player.' Well, I've known Richard all my life as well, so I told Kelly to get him to come along. And I remember he turned up looking like Axl Rose. Richard always looked like the Guns N' Roses singer, as he had hair down to the top of his chest. And he came in, played his bass and made a thunderous noise.

Richard had made a huge impression on Stuart and Kelly. It spelt the end of Mark Everett's tenure with the band.

I remember saying to Kelly, 'We've got to get Mark Everett out of the band! This isn't going to work. Rich is the man for us.' So that's what we went and did. Naughty really, but it had to be done. Then we toyed with the idea of having another guitar player to fill out the sound. We went through three, believe it or not! First we started off with the guy who ended up being Kelly's guitar tech for 10 years, Simon Collier. He now works for my new band Killing For Company. Then we went to another guy and his name was Richard Jones also. So we had two Richard Joneses in the band. Finally, we ended up with the guy we wanted. The first two we weren't happy with, because they didn't quite fit. So we tried out this last guy as we'd heard he was a good guitar player.

And to be honest with you, the Stereophonics would have been a four piece. He joined and we loved him, but he left! He left us! We were all totally happy with him in the band. He was a great guitar player and he did some great backing vocals with Kelly. He was a singer/songwriter in the band he'd been in before, so we now had two people in the band who were writing complementary stuff. But six months before we signed our record deal, he told us that he didn't want to do it any more. It's bizarre, because he played harmonica on one of the songs on our third album called 'Rooftop'. He does this harmonica solo at the end of the track. After he did it, he was just sitting there in the studio, gutted. He said, 'All my mates take the piss out of me for quitting the band!' And I said, 'Well, it's stupid, because we could have been a four piece. You could have been part of the band!' His name was Glenn Hyde. He was from Merthyr Tydfil. He was a lovely guy as well. One of the funniest men I've met in my life. And that was the great thing about him. He just fitted in perfectly. We were all happy with the way he played guitar and we were happy with him as a person. I don't know why he left. It's strange. Just bizarre. And to this day, he can't answer that question as to why he left.

As we stroll across the road from the community centre, I ask Stuart how well this final line-up of the band gelled.

Well, we were becoming a fantastic unit. We were full of determination and we really wanted to do this, no matter what, even if it took every last drop of blood – every last beat of the heart. Whatever it took! And I think that's what set us apart from every other band in the valleys. There were a lot of other bands coming through who were the same age as us. But we were just such a great live band that we just blew everyone else away. For a three-piece band, we made such a noise. But the one thing that I think we had over everyone else – and I'll say this to the day I die and I don't get on well with Kelly now but – the one thing we had over other bands was that no bugger could sing like him. No one at all. Kelly sounded like he was straight from America. Top notch. He sounded like John Fogerty. He sounded like Creedence Clearwater Revival. He sounded like a man, not a little boy! And that was the main thing. He could sing anyone off the stage, and he still can to this day. I've never heard Kelly hit a bum or a flat note, and he's been doing it since he was twelve. Very early on, he could sing rock 'n' roll in the same key as Robert Plant. And that's the truth! But he was only thirteen at the time! [Stuart chuckles at the memory.] He used to say 'My head does hurt a bit after I sing like Plant.' But that was a key thing.

Also when the songwriting side picked up, I think the one thing that moved us on was the influence of a Canadian band called The Tragically Hip. We stumbled across them through a mate of mine called Julian Castaldi. We played a cover of 'Blow at High Dough' from their first album *Up to Here*. They had great lyrics like 'shot a movie in my home town'. It felt right to us, and similar to this place where we were from. Anyway, I remember we had this really big gig coming up in a circus tent just down the road from here in Aberdare. All the local bands had been asked to come. Bizarrely enough, we were called Blind Faith at that time, because we couldn't think of another name. I thought 'Well I know there's an old band with the same name, but what can we do?' We went and played there, opening up with 'Blow at High Dough'. And you know how the song opens up and the big chord eventually comes in? It's very impressive. Well, we had two guitar players at the time, and I remember coming off stage, and every member of every single band were just stood there like that! [Stuart turns to me and Andrew and does the 'jaw dropped' pose.] 'They just stood there nodding and muttering "Bloody hell". They asked me and Kelly if it was our song and we both nodded together and said 'Yeah, too right! Of course it's bloody ours!'

Only a little lie. Well, a massive one, really, I suppose but, to us, we'd discovered something special in The Tragically Hip and I thought we had a blueprint there. We looked into it and that's when Kelly – and I've got to be honest and I think he'll admit it as well – that lyrically, and from a storytelling point of view, The Tragically Hip singer, Gordon Downie, is a massive influence on Kelly Jones. Without a shadow of a doubt! Especially on our first record. The small town kind of stories. Even when I listen to it now, I can hear so much of The Tragically Hip in *Word Gets Around*. And, ironically, we've now become very good friends with the band. We used to stay at their homes whenever we went to Toronto. We went down to their studio. We played ice hockey with them on Lake Ontario. We used to look up to this band, like you wouldn't believe. Now we're friends with them. We went to see them at Cardiff University on the Fully Completely tour in 1992 and I remember forging a student's pass, because only students could get in. So we faked some. It was just £2.50 to get in. £2.50 man! Wow. You could see The Tragically Hip for £2.50. Amazingly, I saw them up in London two years ago and they're still a great live band. They're still a great influence, even with the new band, Killing For Company, and the songs I do with Greg Jones, our lead singer. Greg's really into them and particularly into Gordon Downie.

Gordon's timeless. I think it's something I could even give to my little boy, Cian – if he was eighteen, or nineteen, and in a band. I'd say 'Have a listen to this. It's really cool.' And I think it would still be relevant. So we had a lucky find there.

So The Tragically Hip, AC/DC and Rush were among the prominent musical influences. But I ask Stuart if any friends, or family members, had a big influence on him.

The person who got me into music was my brother, who had a big record collection. He hated me playing records from it. He hated me just looking at it, I should imagine. My brother was a big Rush fan. Obviously you don't do what your brother does. You've got to be different, so I became a big AC/DC fan. But the first album I ever bought was *Deep Purple in Rock*, the gatefold album. I still have it now actually. I bought it when I was about eleven, in a music shop in Aberdare for about three pounds. That was my big love: AC/DC. Then when I got older, I started listening to Rush.

Stuart now reflects on the musical inspiration for his former band-mates.

No one pushed Kelly into music, even though his father was a singer. He asked for a guitar because he wanted to play it. And I borrowed fifty quid from my brother for a drum kit. My mother came home, and straight away she ordered me to get the drums out of her house. [He laughs.] But I managed to persuade her to keep them and thank God I did. As for Richard, I don't think his family were big into music. I don't think most of them owned any records, or listened to any. I think his mother liked Elvis a little and his father kind of liked David Bowie, but nothing major. As for Richard himself, he just jumped onto the bandwagon with us really. Obviously, both Kelly and I were big AC/DC fans. Massive AC/DC fans. We worshipped the ground they walked on. Then another big album which comes to mind is Pearl Jam's *Ten*. When that came out it was a big turning point for us as well. If you look at early pictures of the Stereophonics, we even look like Pearl Jam. I still love that album, *Ten*, to this day. I still play 'Black' on my radio show for Kerrang in Birmingham. In fact, thinking about it, I'll play it tonight. It's timeless. Perfect. So that was our musical heritage.

Now Andrew chips in with a question. He lowers his camera and asks Stuart how much he thought the small-town tales in the band's lyrics contributed to the band's early success.

Yeah, I'm trying to think what was out around the time of our first album and, to be honest with you, there was nothing like what the Stereophonics was doing. Placebo were out there, but they were not really writing lyrics like Kelly. His lyrics were just like mini-films really, weren't they? Obviously, you have to look back at our influences. Bob Dylan was a big influence. There was a guy called Graham Davies at the Ivy Bush pub. He is a big Dylan fan. He used to push a lot of Dylan onto us, and for a great reason. So that's where the Dylan side came from and we were heavily involved into the lyrics. We'd sit there listening, saying 'This is bloody great'. Then when writing, we'd mix it up with stuff from The Tragically Hip and a bit of tongue in cheek from Bon Scott, and create the Stereophonics' sound. No one was doing it out there, the way we were.

I walk alongside Stuart and ask him if, by this time, the band were becoming 'local heroes'? He smiles at the question.

No way! Far from it! Everybody used to say to us 'You'll never be bloody famous! You're not from London!' We thought that didn't matter. Well, I mean does it? But every now and again, there'd be doubts and we'd think 'Are they right?' We'd had this concerted effort of assaulting London back then, for some reason. We'd go, play there, sleep on floors at our mates' houses and then drive back the next morning. Sometimes that was funny. Like when we were on the toll bridge on the M4 coming back from London to Wales. I had an old British Telecom van. As we approached the toll bridge, we'd be desperately scraping the cash together. On the bridge, you have to pay more for a van than for a car. But we'd pull up into the lane where you just throw the correct amount, in coins, into the electronic basket. But we'd only chuck in enough money for a car, not a van, and then we'd drive off double quick, because we didn't have any more money.

But most people didn't think we'd make it big. Not everybody. Usually those who were supportive were our friends and family. But now . . . well, bloody hell! We've put this village on the map. French, Italian, Japanese. All sorts come here to visit, because of us. That caused a stir for a while. It was mad. I don't come up here a huge amount any more. Just if my mates are going out, or watching the rugby. But it's bizarre, because the guy who's the landlord of that place [Stuart points across the road to the club] Fred, he's hilarious. He tells me all the time that he's had all these foreign people around. And he takes them in and gives them food. These French girls will be asking 'Where does Stuart live?' and he'll show them the street. My mum will take them in, make them tea and talk them to death! But, yeah, it was one of those things. Everyone had this impression that we couldn't become famous, because of the area we came from. To many people, this is a shit-hole. Nobody cares about this place! This was built for the pits and the pits are gone. So success was never on the cards in the eyes of most people. They used to say to us 'It's never gonna happen. You've not got enough talent. You'll never be on Top of the Pops!'

And lo and behold, we did it. But the strangest thing about it all is that when we signed the record deal, and made and released our first record, we toured off the back of it. Later, when the tour was over, we said 'We should go back home and write some new songs. Let's go back to the youth club again and rehearse there.' But we couldn't get in! It was fully booked! There were bands everywhere. A few years earlier, we were the only band in Cwaman. But when we came home, we couldn't move for bands. There were nearly twenty-four groups here, which was great really because it got the kids off the streets and stopped them becoming dickheads. That was quite funny.

Stuart looks back at the community centre once more. He's enjoying this trip down memory lane.

This reminds me, the other thing was, at this time, we'd go out to play gigs and nobody scared us. It didn't matter who they were. We knew we could wipe the floor with most bands. Nobody scared us! Whoever we played with, or whoever we supported, we didn't care. We knew we'd win over 50 per cent of their fans. That's how the band became popular. That's how we won so many awards for being the best live band. The Q awards, the Kerrang awards. I see those awards and I feel satisfied because the people voted for them by going to the gigs to see us. You can't really get much better than that, can you? All in all it was a nice little package.

At this point, I tell Stuart that Andrew and I saw him play with the Stereophonics when they were supporting James back in December 1998.

'Oh my God! Really?' replies Stuart, strangely amazed that anyone had seen him play.

'At Wembley Arena,' confirms Andrew.

'Yeah! That was a good tour,' Stuart says, thinking back to what was James's *Greatest Hits* tour, where a packed Wembley was thrilled by the Manchester band's classics such as 'Sit Down', 'Come Home', 'She's a Star' and 'Born of Frustration'. The Stereophonics were supporting them, playing songs from their debut album *Word Gets Around*. The band were very well received by the Wembley crowd.

I tell Stuart my memories of that gig.

It's usual that when a support band comes on, the arena is half empty as people chat, go on a search for beer and drinks, or head for the toilet. But this was one of the few occasions where people actually started coming into the venue once they'd heard the opening bars of the first song. It was 'A Thousand Trees', I think. Andrew and I went to the gig because we both loved James and we'd both bought – and really liked – the first Stereophonics album.

'That's a slight lie, Jeff!' interrupts Andrew with a big grin. 'You taped the Stereophonics album for me!'

'Oh no!' says Stuart, putting his hand to his mouth in mock shock as I'm caught out in my illegal home-taping scam. 'That's not nice. That's not good at all!'

'Oh no. It is good,' insists Andrew, not letting this embarrassing topic drop. I half expect to have to get my wallet out and pay Stuart the lost royalties on the spot to make amends for my past bootlegging ways, no matter how well intentioned they were.

But Andrew explains further.

Jeff did tape it for me and I thought 'Wow. This is a great album.' Then, when we saw you guys live, you were so good and the songs sounded even better live, after the gig, I went out and bought your album on CD. That's how good you played that night at Wembley!

'Good man!' says Stuart, slapping Andrew on the back. That gesture suggests that all is forgiven and I can rest easy and not worry about having conned the band out of the cost of a meal. The Stereophonics didn't go hungry thanks to my home taping. Actually it led to a sale for the band. Perhaps I should ask for commission, I think to myself.

'Yeah. That's how good a live band we were. Absolutely!'

Stuart seems pleased to have his conviction that the Stereophonics were a great live band validated by this story.

That was always the ethic. It's because we grew up listening to the bands like AC/DC and Rush. They were all great live bands and had a great work ethic. There was no shirking. There was no place to hide. With Rush, I remember owning their live video *Exit Stage Left*. Watching it I thought 'Bloody hell!' You could see it was all live. There were no overdubs added onto it. You can see that they are just playing. That's how good they are! And you aspire to become that good, don't you? We used to watch some bands, and we'd want to be as good, if not better, than them. Some people spend more time on getting the right look, or the right haircut, rather than learning to play guitar!

I agree with Stuart. There is nothing worse than seeing a band you like, only to be disappointed when you see them live. The likes of Yes and Rush are note-for-note perfect live. On albums like *Exit Stage Left*, the songs are often better live than they are in the studio. It can be a real letdown when bands sound poor live and they can easily lose an audience that way, I tell Stuart. He agrees.

Definitely. We always thought we were a better live band. Better than we were in the studio. But that's the case with every rock band that has a lot of energy, isn't it? It's very difficult to capture that on record. I still think to this day that most bands can't do it. They can't cut it live. I don't know why! In the studio, it doesn't matter if you make a mistake. You can stop, go back and do it again. But when you're on stage, you're flying by the seat of your pants. Thousands of people have paid a lot of money to see you and you've got to turn it on. You've got to be good. It doesn't matter if you've just argued with your girlfriend, or your mother, or father. You go into your drawer, pull out your best smile, get on stage and entertain.

We now return to the topic of the band's live performances back in 1991. The band had named themselves Tragic Love Company.

Yeah, that name came from three of our favourite bands. We started by taking the words Tragic from The Tragically Hip, Love from Mother Love Bone, and Company from Bad Company. I don't know why we did it. It was a bizarre thing. To me, I still to this day, think the coolest band name in the world is The Tragically Hip. You can never get better than that! But you know what it's like. You're just clutching at straws to get a name. We went through a whole load. But we finally settled on Tragic Love Company. Then someone pointed out to us that the band's name stood for TLC – as in the phrase 'tender loving care'! So first we were Zephyr. Next we became Blind Faith for a while and then we changed to Tragic Love Company and finally to Stereophonics.

'So where did you get the name Stereophonics?' I ask Stuart.

We became the Stereophonics in 1995. We were asked to do a thing called the Splash Tour. It consisted of signed bands at the time, such as the Manic Street Preachers, Catatonia, the 60 Foot Dolls and the Super Furry Animals. This guy had gotten these four bands together to play in four different parts of south Wales. One was in the Muni in Pontypridd.

23

Another was in the Coliseum just outside Aberdare. One was in Newport and I can't remember where the final one was, actually. He put an advert in the newspapers asking for local support bands. So our night saw us supporting Catatonia. I think they had just been signed and had released an EP, or maybe their first album. So we got a phone call from the promoter, Wayne Coleman. He called my mum's house. She answered the phone and told me that some guy called Wayne was on the phone wanting to talk to me. We had sent them a tape of two songs. The tape had mine and Kelly's phone numbers and house addresses on. It would have been two songs: 'Tramp's Vest' and 'Local Boy'. So Wayne phoned and asked me how long we'd been playing together and how many members we had in the band. He said that our tape had blown him away and that it was the best demo tape he'd heard in ten years! I thought he was joking. But he said to me, 'Can I just ask you one thing? Can you change your name? The one you have is terrible! Tragic Love Company. It's awful. I want you to play with Catatonia. The gig's in two weeks' time, but I want you to change your name. You've got five days to come up with a new name because that's when I'm printing the posters!'

Well, we sat in the pub for like four days. At one point, Kelly wanted to call the band Mabel Cable: my mother's name. He'd even drawn logos on beer mats for Mabel Cable. Can you believe it? We were coming close to this deadline and the promoter was ringing me up every other day asking 'Have you got a name for the band yet?' I'd tell him 'No' and he'd say, 'You've got to get a name. You guys are going to be huge. The songs are great.'

Well, the next day, I was in my mum's house. My father – who died when I was ten – used to own lots of old 45s. My mother had bought him, as a present for his fortieth birthday, this stereogram. It was a piece of furniture. You pull the front panel down on some brass hinges and inside is the stereo. It was all black. In fact, my mother's still got it in the house and if you want to go see it, I'm sure she'd let you. So I was sitting on the bed. My brother had a bass guitar in there. I was sitting on his bed and I just looked down at the stereogram and saw the words 'Falcon Stereophonic'. I thought 'Ah. That's pretty cool! Stereophonics.' I said it again and then said it once more. My mother now tells a story about how I came running down the stairs shouting 'Yeah I've got it. I've got the name.' Well, I didn't come running down the stairs shouting like that. Honest! I simply walked down calmly and went straight to Kelly's house down the road, and I asked him, 'What do you think of Stereophonics?' I told him I got it from my father's stereogram and he thought it was great. Kelly was in art college at the time. So he went to college the next day and designed and drew the logo. So later that day, we phoned the guy up and he said 'Brilliant. You're on the bill.' That was the actual start of the Stereophonics.

4

THE ROAD TO A RECORD DEAL

Kelly's mother answered the phone. This voice said, 'Hello I'm Richard Branson.' And she replied, 'Well, I'm Elizabeth Taylor.' And he went 'No. I'm really Richard Branson and I want to speak to Kelly Jones!'

Stuart Cable, Cwmaman, August 2007

SATURDAY, 2 MARCH 1996

A poor Welsh rugby team have just been hammered 30 points to 17 at Lansdowne Road in Dublin. Rugby is the lifeblood of Wales, so the mood around Aberdare is grim. It seems another depressing year in the Five Nations rugby championship lies ahead. Wales are going to struggle to do well in this tournament.

At half past five, an hour after the game has ended, the Stereophonics are inside the Coliseum Theatre, ready to play their first gig under their new name. Another band called The Pocket Devils is also on the bill supporting Catatonia. The Pocket Devils feature Glenn Hyde, the guitarist who could have been the fourth member of the Stereophonics a few years earlier, but decided against it.

Opened in 1938, the Coliseum – just outside Aberdare – had been one of the biggest attractions in the south Wales valleys up until the dominance of TV in the 1960s. Now the staple of the theatre is pantomime season. Tonight, though, is the turn of pop and rock music.

Inside the dressing room, the members of the Stereophonics are larking about. Kelly and Stuart are joking around, while Richard Jones sits nearby watching his bandmates with a wry smile on his face. Stuart suddenly decides that the best way to alleviate the boredom, as they wait to go on stage, is to rifle through the dressing room's wardrobe. He opens the door and plucks out the first thing to hand: a green dress. 'This would look good on you, Rich!' he jokes. The drummer puts the dress back and flicks through hanger after hanger of stage gear used by the actors during dramatic productions at the Coliseum. Suddenly Stuart strikes gold. He pulls out a fur coat. 'Bloody hell! Look at this, guys.' Kelly now takes a closer interest in the drummer's clothes hunt. 'Let's have a go at that fur coat,' he asks. 'It's wicked!' So the Stereophonics frontman puts on the old fur coat and models it for his two best friends. 'Wow, you look good,' Stuart informs him. 'You should wear it on stage!' Kelly gives Stuart a look as if to say, 'Are you mad?' He looks at himself again in the mirror. 'It's a bit smelly,' he moans.

'Don't worry, man. Just wear it. You'll knock 'em dead,' encourages Stuart.

So the band takes to the stage with Kelly wearing the old, battered and just a little bit smelly fur coat. They play a 40-minute set, unaware that this performance is about to change their lives forever. Sitting in the audience watching closely is John Brand. He's here to give a seminar on how to get a record deal. With him in the audience are representatives from a couple of record companies, who are here to see The Pocket Devils. They are being tipped as the hot new band. But John has been won over instead by the Stereophonics' unique sound. After their short set, Stuart, Kelly and Richard are back in the dressing room, congratulating themselves on a great performance. 'Let's see Catatonia follow that,' says Stuart in buoyant mood. Like the rest of the band, he's not in awe of any headline act.

It's then that the dressing-room door bursts open. 'Have you got management?' asks a strange-looking man, panting for breath. He doesn't bother with an introduction.

'No', say the band in unison, taken aback by the bluntness of the opening question.

'Well, thank fuck for that!' exclaims the stranger.

The Stereophonics exchange bemused glances. Who is this bizarre man with a pronounced English accent?

They decided to find out. 'Who the hell are you?' Stuart asks him equally as bluntly.

'Sorry. I'm John Brand,' says the man proffering a hand. 'I would like to be your manager. Have you got a demo tape?'

Again, the dumbfounded band answer in unison. 'Yes.'

John Brand now turns his attention to Kelly Jones. 'Where did you get that fur coat from? It's bloody brilliant! Now can you all come to Chieveley services on the M4 on Monday morning? I want to meet up with you.'

'We've got things to do, but we can move them to meet you there,' says Stuart.

With that, John Brand is gone and the Stereophonics are left scratching their heads and wondering where this will take them.

MONDAY MORNING, 4 MARCH 1996

The band is sitting in the food area of Chieveley Services on junction 13 of the M4 motorway from Wales to London. They're joined by John Brand who, after the greetings are dispensed with, starts the conversation with his typical direct approach.

'So have you had any interest from any record companies?'

The band admit that they've nothing concrete.

'OK,' replies Brand. 'Just leave it with me. I guarantee that in just three weeks' time, you'll have every record company in this country wanting to sign you!'

Two and a half weeks later, John has been true to his word. More than thirty record companies are queuing up to sign this Welsh trio. John Brand's phone hasn't stopped ringing. He organizes a number of meetings with all the companies who've approached him, hungry to get the right deal for the band. Many of these companies are the same ones who just months earlier had sent the Stereophonics rejection letters. Thanks, but no thanks! Now, a short time later, it's a totally different story.

For the next eighteen months, John makes Kelly wear that fur coat at every gig. It had proved a lucky find.

JUNE 2007, CWMAMAN

Stuart, Andrew and I have left the community centre where the band used to rehearse many moons ago. We're now sitting just down the road, in the bar at the Cwmaman Institute. It's soft drinks all around. Stuart sits sipping a lemonade, as does Andrew to his right. I'm sitting to Stuart's left with an orange juice and soda. We're surrounded by shelves of sporting memorabilia: signed Cardiff City football shirts, sporting photos and autographed rugby tops. 'I got that one for the club,' says Stuart proudly pointing at the Welsh international top. The rugby jersey's been signed by top Welsh players of the 1990s, including Alan Bateman, Neil Jenkins and Rob Howley. The names of the three Stereophonics are also scrawled proudly at the top of the famous red shirt.

Changing the subject, Stuart laughs at the memory of that gig in Aberdare, long ago, which changed the band's fortunes.

I wonder if Kelly's still got that fur coat? It's just strange how those events happen really. Like the change of name, going to that gig in Aberdare, finding the fur coat and John turning up at the gig. Kelly also wore that coat at a gig we did at The Filling Station in Newport for all the record companies who were interested in us. You've got to remember that everybody thinks that the band's success is down to writing great songs – and of course 90 per cent of it is. But I reckon a big percentage of it is down to how clever your manager is. And John was such a clever bugger! He just turned around and said to us 'I want you to become big fish in a small pond. You need to become massive in Wales. Then just let the rest of the country follow on. And this is what we're going to do. We're going to play a show in Newport at The Filling Station. I'm going to make every record company in London come to watch you in Wales. We're not going to go to them!'

We told him that it would never work. But we were wrong. So wrong! They all came. There were 52-seater buses coming down from London and every record company in the UK was at that gig. Everybody! I'll give you an example. We had the guys from Polydor Records travel down here to see us. They wanted to take us to a restaurant.' We told them, 'There is no restaurant in Cwmaman! But we can go for fish and chips at the chip shop, or to the pub. That's about it.'

Well they said 'What about Aberdare?' We all sniggered 'No, not really.' So we ended up going down to Cardiff instead. It was just totally bizarre. You wouldn't believe what was happening. They all wanted to come here. To see Cwmaman.

Stuart pauses and looks out of the window of the institute. You can see down the valley to the massive mountain overlooking the village. He takes a sip from his drink and places it back on the small, wobbly circular table in front of us.

The ones who wanted it the most were V2 Records: Richard Branson's mob. They kept knocking. They wanted it big time and would come to every gig we played.

I ask Stuart if it's true that Branson himself rang the band from a Caribbean island.

Yeah. And Kelly's mother answered the phone. This voice said, 'Hello I'm Richard Branson.' And she replied 'Well, I'm Elizabeth Taylor.' And he went 'No. I'm really Richard Branson and I want to speak to Kelly!' So after this, Kelly dashes around to my house and says 'You'll never guess what! Richard Branson's just phoned me. He says that he wants to sign the band as he's heard so many good reports about us. He's promised to put a lot of money behind us and says V2 will be 101 per cent there for us. We are their number one priority.'

Kelly was right. Branson gave us his personal guarantee that he would make this work and his label would back us big time.

So in August 1996, the Welsh three piece headed down to London for the day to sign on the dotted line. It's rumoured that afterwards the band headed for Oxford Street to go on a shopping spree.

Stuart laughs as he remembers the day the band finally had some money to its name.

Oh God. We had £247,000 in cheque form. Then we all had £1,000 each in cash. So we headed straight for Oxford Street and bought some clothes. It was the first pair of Levi 501s I've owned in my life. I mean, it's really weird to look back at it now. But we didn't earn much back then. I was lucky if I had £35 in my pocket, and I probably had to give £15 of that to my mother. Obviously you'd save some to go out on the weekend. So really, we lived from hand to mouth. Yeah, I remember it took me ten weeks to spend that thousand pounds.

As Andrew saunters up to the bar to grab another round of soft drinks, I ask Stuart how the band had made a living in the run-up to being signed by Branson.

Oh yes – we worked right up to the signing. Kelly worked on a vegetable stall at the weekends, and was in college during the week. Richard's father had a scaffolding business. So Richard was the one who used to earn all the money. It was a decent wage for a boy of his age, though it was a hard job. Then I had to find myself a job that earned a reasonable amount of money, but was also flexible enough to allow me to go back and forth to London. Eventually this job came up, which fitted the bill. It was delivering school dinners. I would start at 10.30 in the morning and finish at 2.30 in the afternoon. It was perfect, because I could head down for a gig in London in the afternoon, stay the night and leave early at six the next morning to come home and be in work by half past ten. And that's what we all used to do. Obviously Richard was quite flexible timewise, because his father owned the business. Kelly was also flexible, because of college, as long as he got his work done! So I was the only problem. But I took this job. And well . . .

Stuart pauses for a while and a bright smile flickers across his face.

I'll never forget this as long as I live, but there was this woman at work called Veronica. I can't remember her surname. She was the big, big boss. What a bloody nasty piece of work, though. I used to have really long hair back then and I would wear my hat backwards. At the end of the day, I was of the view that if you got your work done and you did it properly, then people couldn't criticize you. But she used to have a right go at me, finding anything she could to moan about, whether it was my hair, work or whatever. I remember she often used to stand outside having a cigarette, and would be there when we were taking the school dinners out at eleven o'clock. We'd take out the whole run and we had about six schools each. We'd drop all the food off, so it would be ready then for the kids to eat. Now I remember we were standing outside and she said to me 'What's this I've been hearing about you going back and forward to London?' So I said to her 'Yeah, we are. It looks like we're gonna sign a record deal.' So she looked me up and down and said 'You'll be bloody back in six months.' Like hell, I thought.

He laughs again.

I should have gone back to see her once we were big. But attitudes have changed now, particularly round this neck of the woods. We were the first success story from here, weren't we? And that's the other thing I love about this place – and is why I come back here – and why I've lived here so long and still have a lot of friends here. It's because it brings you right back down to earth and makes you remember that you're just one of the boys. You're just a normal human being. Don't get above your station. That's why it's good to come back here. I like it.

Andrew has started taking photographs from the bar of me and Stuart. He breaks off and tells Stuart that it must be easy when you've had success to live in a cocoon, lose touch with your friends and just do the things that rich people do.

'Yeah. Yeah,' agrees Stuart waving to two of the locals who've just walked in.

You can indeed, and that's not the kind of life I want to lead really. I wanted to have children and I wanted to bring them up in Wales, to be Welsh. I've always – and still to this day – had this thing about London, which I don't particularly like. You don't know who your friends are there. If something happened up this neck of the woods, though, everyone would know about it the next day. We'd know who did it, what time it was done, and how many of them were there and I think that's good in itself. I know it's kind of self-policing in its own way, but my mother still lives here and I know that if anything happened to her, I'd know straight away. Same as my brother. Even where I'm living now it's exactly the same. Although three or four miles away, there's still that sense of community there.

As we prepare to leave, Stuart breaks off to talk to the two men at the bar, who'd waved to him on the way in. The three exchange handshakes, all smiling and laughing. Stuart is an immensely popular figure in this area.

As we walk out, Stuart returns to the subject of the band's first record deal. When Richard Branson sold his first record company, Virgin, to EMI for £560 million in 1992, he promised not to set up in competition for at least three years. As good as his word he waited four years, then he started his second record company, V2. The Stereophonics were his first signing.

He'd sold Virgin Records and bought the airline, which made him most of his money. I don't think the first record label ever really made him that much money, until he sold it! It was a bit of a strange one, because what he went and did then with V2 was very clever. They set up regional promotion teams. So it meant rather than someone from London speaking to a radio station in, say, Bradford and having no relationship with them at all, they had local people to cover different areas. They would allocate regions of 300 miles and tell their rep, 'Right here's your car, here's your product and here's your band.' And that's what we did for three months. We sat in trains, and in the smallest cars you've seen in your life, travelling the UK with these reps. I don't know what they were, these cars, but obviously Branson had bought them at a knockdown price. They were tiny. We worked closely with Jo Hunt in Wales – where she was the regional girl – and she's now our manager in Killing For Company.

I'm a firm believer that that's what broke the band. It was the knowledge and hard work of the people at V2. They knew all the right people at the FM radio stations. They'd walk in and say, 'I've got this great new band. You've got to play them. You know that I'm a good judge of a band.' And, sure enough, the radio presenters would play our records because they had a level of trust in the reps. The bizarre thing was that John Brand's original idea of being big in Wales first was a bit mad, because we actually became bigger in Scotland than we did in our home country. And in a much quicker timescale. We were playing big venues in Scotland, while still playing much smaller places in Wales. But that's the Scottish for you. They love their rock music! I remember Rush mentioned the audience when they recorded a few songs on their live album *Exit Stage Left* in Glasgow.

We all stop walking for a moment. 'That's right,' I tell Stuart. 'I had that album too as a teenager. Rush actually credited the audience in Glasgow with "backing vocals" on the song "Closer to the Heart" in the sleeve notes.'

Stuart chips in with the song title – 'Closer to the Heart' – exactly as I say it!

Yeah that's right. I remember those sleeve notes. Do you know, it's like the first time we went on stage in Glasgow and I could only just hear Kelly sing the opening verse of 'A Thousand Trees', with just him and a guitar. The audience sang it as loud as hell. The hairs on the back of my neck went up. I thought 'Wow. What's going on here.' Then on the song 'Traffic', they sang the bit where the bass and drums drop out and Kelly sings his part alone. That was quite scary. As a drummer, I didn't know what to do. Obviously, I took my cues from Kelly as he leads that section. So if I couldn't hear his voice and his guitar, I was screwed! I couldn't see his mouth moving, because he was facing away from me. I'm looking at Richie on bass, and he's looking at me and shrugging. Luckily we came back in at the right place.

We pause again as Stuart spots some old friends at the roadside on the way back to where our cars are parked. One of them has a new motorbike. Stuart loves bikes. The three chat about Harley Davidsons and taking a road trip somewhere. Despite his success, people here still view him the same as before. It's Stuart Cable! He's one of us.

5

WORD GETS AROUND

We'd send tapes away in Chinese food cartons. Then we'd send the next tapes away in old shoes . . . The poor woman in the post office used to look at us as if we were stupid when we used to turn up with all these different things. It was anything really just to get people's attention.

Stuart Cable, Cwmaman, June 2007

It's a sunny June day in Cwmaman. I've spent the morning here with Stuart Cable trying to map his journey, with his former band the Stereophonics, from an unknown Welsh mining village to major super-stardom.

It's a fascinating journey. Stuart is an entertaining raconteur with a limitless supply of humorous tales about the rocky road to success. We look down the road past the nearby football field and toward the small community centre, where the fledgling band used to rehearse. Once again, we start walking towards the small building and stop just outside it, by the village's main bus stop.

Back in 1996, as soon as the Stereophonics had signed for V2 Records, they set about putting together their debut album. Many of the songs had already been written here in Cwmaman, with most of those put together by the band at this very community centre. Some of the lyrics for the songs from that first album were inspired by things clearly visible from the centre.

'The one thing that springs to my mind,' says Stuart, 'is that we were here one Sunday morning rehearsing, when this old guy, Billy Davey, walked down the road. I turned to Kelly and asked him, "Have you heard the story about his daughter?" And he said "No. What story's that?"'

So I told him that she'd committed suicide. She jumped off the Severn Bridge on the M4 motorway and into the River Severn. The next day Kelly had written a song called 'Billy Davey's Daughter'. But when we recorded the first album, Billy Davey didn't want us to use his name. So we tried for four days to rework it with different words, which sounded the same, such as Milly Navy. But in the end, it was just never going to work. So I said, 'Boys, we've just got to bite the bullet and do it.' Luckily, we knew someone, a friend of ours, who also knew Billy quite well. He went up to see Billy and told him 'Well, look. The song's not anything to take the piss out of your daughter. It's an absolute tribute to her memory. You should listen carefully to the words.' So we gave him a copy of the lyrics, and after he saw those and realized our intentions were good, he gave us his consent. I can still see him now. We were sitting here in the community centre and we could see Bill Davey walking past. He's dead now, God bless his soul. But I just remember him walking past, then telling the story to Kelly and, hey presto, he'd written a song about it the next day. You never think in a million years that you're going to play gigs and tens of thousands of people are gonna sing those words back to you. It's totally bizarre. Then obviously there were the Billy Dunn gates over there, which were pulled down.

Stuart points down the road to the field just beyond the community centre. Billy Dunn was a respected sports coach, who saw his career ruined following an alleged sexual encounter with a female student. The gates on the sports ground had been named in honour of him and his work in the community, but were then pulled down in the wake of the ensuing rumour and scandal.

That's from the song 'A Thousand Trees'. The changing rooms are mentioned in that song. In fact, we're standing by the very bus stop that Kelly mentions in the song's opening line.

As if to remind me and Andrew, Stuart sings the opening two lines:

Standing at the bus stop with my shopping in my hands, when I'm over-hearing elder ladies as the rumours start to fly.

Such a notorious event in a very small, close-knit community was bound to have a massive effect. The spiralling rumours were reflected in Kelly Jones's lyrics in this song, summed up by the lines, 'It only takes one tree to make a thousand matches. It only takes one match to burn a thousand trees.'

Stuart now points toward the former Double Decker club – just opposite the community centre.

We also wrote about Rhydian, who worked there. He's in the song 'Goldfish Bowl'. It's the line 'Redhead, gingerbread, sells tickets at the door'. When they put bands on in Cwmaman, he used to be the man who sat on the door. He's got a big red beard. So that's where Kelly got the line from. 'Goldfish Bowl' also features the character Caramel Crisp. He's my mother's next-door neighbour, Mel Crisp. He's a pigeon fancier. I still don't know why they call them 'fanciers'. It's a bit bizarre to me.

Also on 'Goldfish Bowl' is the line: 'The Kingfishers' lead singer calms his nerves.' That's about Kelly's father. He was a singer in a band called the Kingfishers.

And from the same song, 'Cliff Chips lines up his dominos'. Now Cliff Chips was the landlord of the Ivy Bush pub, our local. So all these little characters appear, because that's what the song is about. Cwmaman is a goldfish bowl. It can be the best place in the world to live. It can be the worst. You don't wanna go shag your best mate's girlfriend, because he's gonna find out.

Stuart lets out another huge laugh. It's not very often you find Stuart in a bad mood. He enjoys company and he's been revelling in telling Andrew and me about the Stereophonics' beginnings. We say our goodbyes and agree to meet up in a few days. Andrew takes a handful of photographs of Stuart, posing outside the front of his mother's house. We shake hands and head our separate ways.

5 JULY 2007, ABERDARE

Just down the road from Cwmaman is Stuart's home on the outskirts of Aberdare. Andrew and I park outside, where we're greeted by Stuart and two rather big rottweiler-type dogs. First, we walk across the garden to another, smaller building, which doubles up as a rehearsal studio for Stuart's new band. Upstairs is a room in which Stuart keeps all his gold and platinum discs. 'Wow,' I say. 'This is incredible. There are a whole lot of memories up here.' Just above a bar area built into the room, there's a recreation of the cover of the Stereophonics' third album *Just Enough Education to Perform*. But this time the wording on the cover says 'Cable Castle Inn' in reference to his home. As I look around at the discs and awards, Stuart casually hands me something before disappearing into the next room. It's a Brit Award! The one the Stereophonics won for 'Best Newcomer' in 1998. I quickly recover, and cheekily pose with the award, getting Andrew to take a photograph of me holding it!

I put the Brit Award down on the pool table in the middle of the room, and head next door with Andrew to catch up with Stuart. In the next room, there are more photographs on the wall. Stuart posing with

Led Zeppelin's Jimmy Page is one that catches my eye. Plus the room is full of drum kits. 'Goodness. How many kits did you need?' I ask.

'Well,' says Stuart. 'After every album, or before every tour, Yamaha used to ring me up and offer me a new drum kit. I'd be a fool to refuse, wouldn't I?'

Tour over, we head across the back garden and into the house. Simon Collier, the Stereophonics's former guitar tech, has just arrived. Stuart makes him a cup of tea as Simon skims through today's newspaper.

Then we move through into the living room to discuss the recording of the Stereophonics's first album. With many of the songs already written, the band now needed to put them on tape. One of the recording studios they chose was the legendary Rockfield. As a Welsh band, they had to try out one of the world's most famous studios, which just happens to be based almost on their doorstep.

Word Gets Around

Word Gets Around is the Stereophonics's debut album. It reached number six in the album charts in Britain, making it the only one of the band's first four albums not to reach number one. Many fans, though, consider it to be their best work.

Rockfield is the home of rock legends. Black Sabbath, Queen, Robert Plant, Motörhead, Oasis, The Stone Roses, Rush: the list is almost endless. The Stereophonics wanted to follow in the footsteps of those legendary names.

Obviously, growing up being a big Rush fan, I read the credits on their albums and saw 'Recorded at Rockfield in Monmouth'. I used to think 'There's no way they came to Wales to record that!' But they did. And also John Brand, our manager at the time, engineered those records. In fact he engineered lots of albums at Rockfield. He was saying that we should go down there, because there's a really good vibe. And he was right. We had a great time down there. Especially with the owner Kingsley Ward telling us all the stories of these legendary bands. He told me a great story about Rush, actually. I'd asked him 'What were they like? What were they really like?' And Kingsley said 'They were great. I came back from the shops one day down in town and the guitarist Alex Lifeson and bass player Geddy Lee were painting the windows.'

Can you imagine? They had the gloss paint out. So while Neil Peart was doing some drum edits, his bandmates were painting Rockfield. It's amazing with all the history behind it. It's so cool. I think that's the appeal – that it is so far away from the hustle and bustle. Most of the bands who recorded there came from big cities. You look at all the major bands that were at Rockfield: Queen, Rush, Oasis, The Stone Roses, Sabbath. They were all from major cities. I also think that here in Wales, we don't appreciate what we've got sometimes. I really believe that. The surroundings are wonderful and also there's the thing with Monmouth that nobody bothers you, do they? When we did some pre-production for the third album *Just Enough Education to Perform* at Monnow Valley, which was Rockfield's former rehearsal studio, we used to get people coming over to say hello, but there was no hassle. It's a very friendly town, yet they give you your own space. I've been told stories about the Nag's Head, where Robert Plant used to drink. Can you just imagine going in there in the 80s and there's Planty sitting there going 'Hi. How you doing?'

Stuart suddenly breaks off. 'Wooh!' he says putting his hands on top of his head. 'Sorry about that. Liverpool almost scored.' On the TV, Liverpool are playing the Dutch side Feyenoord in a pre-season football tournament in Amsterdam. Simon wanders in to join the three of us and we watch the next few minutes until half time. Then there's a brief discussion about the latest signing for Cardiff City (Stuart, Andrew and I are all fans of the Bluebirds), who just happens to be former Liverpool legend Robbie Fowler. The former Reds striker was simply called 'God' by the Liverpool faithful. We soon resume our discussion about the Stereophonics' time at Rockfield recording *Word Gets Around*.

Can you imagine going somewhere like that, where you can go and stay for as long as you want, miles away from anywhere, and make as much noise as you want. It was a dream come true. Going there, the owner Kingsley Ward showed us where all the punk bands recorded and where the likes of The Damned and The Stranglers scrawled on the wall. Oh, he said to us, I painted over it! Imagine bands like The Damned writing on the wall, but he just painted over it.

He laughs along with Andrew and Simon at the image. 'Fantastic.'

But the Stereophonics also recorded some of the first album away from Rockfield.

We did half of *Word Gets Around* in a place called Battery Studios in London. It wasn't residential and it was a pain in the arse – if you'll pardon my French. We'd record until the wee hours of the morning. Then, we'd have to get the receptionist at Battery to call a cab to get us back to our digs. When you're in a residential studio, the contrast is so different. It is the best thing in the world. Battery was the only time that we ever recorded non-residential. Ever. After Battery, we went to Rockfield, Monnow Valley and to Hook End Manor in Reading. We also went to Peter Gabriel's Real World in Bath. I think it's the only way to record. You get more done. You wake up in the morning, go downstairs and get your breakfast. You don't have to get a taxi, or a train, or travel across town. I found it very, very appealing.

I ask Stuart if he had any favourite memories from Rockfield.

I think just the history of the place. We had a great time. I remember we had the first mobile phone we'd ever owned when we worked at Rockfield. We decided to get a band mobile phone. In 1996! There weren't many about. That's a strange memory. I don't know why that came into my head. We were all arguing as to who was going to keep the phone. But just sitting down and talking to Kingsley Ward is truly amazing. Probably 90 per cent of my record collection was recorded at Rockfield. So you just sit down, and imagine what Neil Peart must have felt like and Geddy Lee, Alex Lifeson, Roger Taylor and John Bonham. All those legends that graced that studio. Fantastic. The only band I love that didn't record there was AC/DC. Everybody else did. Just looking at the back of those albums, where it says 'Recorded at Rockfield'. Wonderful. I'm still convinced that the *Farewell to Kings* album by Rush is named after Kingsley Ward, because it says lower down in the credits '. . . and a Farewell to Kingsley'. Now, I'm sure they named that album after him. How cool is that? I keep meaning to go back to Rockfield and ask him. I've been recording with the new band in Monnow Valley, so I keep meaning to swing a left, pop in and ask him. I was only reading the cover to *Farewell to Kings* the other day. I got the old vinyl record down to show my little boy. I was looking at the cover again, and there it was '. . . and a Farewell to Kingsley'. Now I must have read that a thousand times as a kid, but it only fitted into relevance since I've been to Rockfield with the Stereophonics and actually met Kingsley. I wouldn't have known who he was years before. But how cool is that if Rush did name it after him?

I tell Stuart that Geddy Lee from Rush once told me the band was chased across a field by some cows on their first day at Rockfield. They knew it was the rural life for them while they recorded there. Rockfield does look more like a farm (which it started as) than a recording studio.

'Yeah, I know,' says Stuart. 'There's just a little green sign that says Rockfield, and pretty much nothing else. It does look like a farm and they've still got horses there. I remember when we first went there, I was following our manager, John Brand, who'd made some records there. And I was thinking, "This can't be the right place. This is somebody's farm!" But it's the perfect retreat for the band who want to get away from everybody, really.'

When the band left the studios they signed the guest book – as everybody does. Rockfield's guestbook should be in a museum. The top of the band's page was scrawled with the words:

7th October 1996. Stereophonics . . . alright or what?

Kelly Jones then wrote 'Thanks for the hospitality, especially the girls in the kitchens.' In smaller letters to the side he scribbled 'Came in with a Gibson S.G. guitar. Went out minus the head!'

That started a theme. Richard Jones simply wrote 'Came in with hair. Left without.' While Stuart's contribution was 'From Cwmaman to Monmouth to ? Thanks everybody.' Then in the corner he added – in keeping the theme started by Kelly – 'Came in with two girlfriends. Left with one.'

That was the Stereophonics's contribution to Rockfield's own hall of fame – its guestbook signed down the years by the likes of Lemmy and Motörhead, Robert Plant, Ozzy Osbourne and Black Sabbath, Queen, Rush and many, many more.

Stuart has also recorded at Monnow Valley Studios, just a mile or so down the road from Rockfield, just outside Monmouth. It used to be called The Old Mill House and was Rockfield's rehearsal studio. But when the owners of Rockfield, Kingsley and Charles Ward, divided the land, Charles turned it into a recording studio in its own right. He renamed it Monnow Valley.

Yeah, we did some pre-production there with the Stereophonics. In a similar way to all the bands in the 70s. That's when Black Sabbath used to write and rehearse at Monnow Valley, and then go and record elsewhere. And, in turn, I myself think there's a better drum room at Monnow Valley than there is at Rockfield. I know some music purists might want to gouge my eyes out for that one, but I really do believe that. We did some pre-production at Monnow Valley for the third album and then went to Real World after that. We went into the number one studio there. Real World is another bizarre studio to say the least. Peter Gabriel has these two studios. Number one is like a proper studio, where you have the glass window separating the control room and the live room. But studio number two is in a big round room, because it's an old mill. So the desk is in the middle of the room and you set up the drums, bass and guitar around it. It's one big room, so you can't hide from anybody. In the end though, I think we did the drums in another room, because there was so much sound spilling through. But, overall, Real World is another great place. Very relaxed, and also difficult to find. It's off the beaten track some five miles away from Bath. On our first trip there, it took us three hours to find the place. We got lost umpteen times. We also used the residential studios at Hook End Manor, which used to be owned by Dave Gilmour from Pink Floyd. Now it's owned by Trevor Horn. I remember going there and that was a great place. It used to be a monastery. It's a fantastic building. You leave the house and walk across the courtyard to get to the studio. We had great fun there, got a lot done and the band and producer really bonded.

Going back to the first album, I ask Stuart how the writing was divided. The album credits both him and Kelly Jones.

Well, I'm sure Kelly will tell you differently. But I used to do a lot with Kelly. I'd arrange the songs, more than anything else. Kelly would usually come up with the initial idea and the lyrics. Now I'm not saying I'm a great arranger, but I seemed to do a lot of that stuff. I have ideas about the way things should be done and be arranged. So I'd sort out the openings to the songs and how they'd end. I'd also organize different parts to fit with Kelly's melody and lyrics. When we first started, it was just Kelly and me. We'd do all the real hard work, like making the posters, putting them up, going down to the local post office with sixty tapes to send away, once a month, to record companies. All the phone numbers on the tapes were either for my house, or Kelly's house. So Richard Jones, our bassist, took a back seat in that respect, really. I should imagine that, because he was the new boy in the band, he left a lot to us. Kelly and I were so focused and determined back then. Pretty scarily so. We knew exactly what we wanted. We'd be in each other's houses every night sitting there thinking about what we could do next. And we'd send tapes away in Chinese food cartons. Then we'd send the next tapes away in old shoes. Then we'd send them in some other bizarre packaging. The poor woman in the post office used to look at us as if we were stupid when we used to turn up with all these different things. It was anything really just to get people's attention.

Once we sat down and said 'Right. This is what we are going to do. We are going to take the guitar solos out of the songs and become like The Kinks. We need short, three-minute, snappy songs to get into the record companies' faces. We're not going to get their attention by drooling long guitar solos in their faces. We can do that in later life, if we get where we're going.' Hence the song 'More Life in a Tramp's Vest'. We had this mindset of doing all we could to get people to notice us. I knew we were a good band. I remember talking to Kelly one day after I'd gone to pick him up from college, as his car had broken down or something. He said 'I've got a song . . .'

Stuart now breaks off to hum and strum out the riff to 'More Life in a Tramp's Vest' with an air guitar.

So Kelly starts singing it. It's all about him working on the market stall. So the next Sunday we went into the studio and recorded it. Kelly and I were friends, like you won't believe. But that's the way it is sometimes in a band. It's like being married.

When *Word Gets Around* was released in 1997, it sold 20,000 copies in its first week. It made number six in the UK album charts and spawned four hit singles: 'A Thousand Trees', 'Traffic', 'More Life in a Tramp's Vest' and 'Local Boy in the Photograph'. The latter song made number fourteen in the UK singles charts. It was a hugely successful debut album.

Soon after, the band started work on its second album, *Performance and Cocktails*. A concert in front of 10,000 people at Cardiff Castle was the landmark point between the release of the first album and the launch of the second.

Yes, that concert was very important at that point. We actually played the song 'The Bartender and the Thief' from the second album that night. We were still in the studio at that time, though, putting the album together. It was very close to completion, because 'The Bartender and the Thief' was one of the last things we did on that album. To be quite honest and frank, and very sad about it all, that was the last song that we ever wrote together in a room as a band. After that, Kelly went on his little way, sat alone in his house, and wanted to sing, write and produce everything. That was very sad. I didn't know it was going to end that way.

Stuart goes quiet as he reflects on the acrimonious way the band ended. It's something he'll open up to me about on later occasions. But now he recollects himself and recalls the Cardiff Castle concert.

So we played 'Bartender' at Cardiff Castle. That gig was yet again a master stroke by our manager John Brand. That started off only because a European Summit was going to happen in Wales. As this summit was coming along, Cardiff Council had granted the use of the castle in the city centre as a live music venue for the first time since the 1970s. So John

Brand – he's always got his finger on the pulse – without telling us, went down to Cardiff and met the council. He told them 'Why don't we have the Stereophonics playing there. They'll pull a huge crowd in Wales. They're a happening band.' The council weren't convinced, but John persuaded them and changed their minds. He went and turned that gig from a council concert into a Stereophonics gig. At first, the council had only wanted 1,500 tickets to be sold. But in the end we sold 10,000 tickets. That man has got to be thanked for opening the door for all the other bands who've gone and played Cardiff Castle recently. But we just thought he was off his trolley. Mad. We told him there was no way that we could sell 10,000 tickets. But he said 'Trust me. It'll happen.' In the end, we could have sold 40,000. We could have done four nights there.

Stuart then remembers the band taking to the stage.

That was another thing. The whole backdrop for the gig. Do you remember? The back of the stage was covered in this silver tape. That was deliberately done to echo what we used to have on the back of the stage, upstairs in the old club we used to play in Cwmaman. It was the look we wanted. We wanted the Castle concert to look like the village's working men's club. It was hilarious when we walked on stage and saw it. 'Bloody hell,' we thought, 'it's a bit bigger than we anticipated.' But that gig was a masterstroke by John Brand, as was the later gig at the Morfa stadium in Swansea, which was also John's brainchild. We played to 50,000 people that night. John's just so clever. He knew the stadium there was going to be demolished very soon, so he went to see Swansea Council and rented it off them for peanuts. Supposedly, it was being torn down the next day, although eighteen months later it was still up. But that didn't matter to us. He was a very shrewd businessman. He knew he had a good product and he knew his selling skills could market us with no worries at all. Now it raises the question, why aren't other managers that good? Maybe it's the rapport. I've see him work. He doesn't raise his voice. He keeps it all on a level. He doesn't get argumentative. He knows how to get a bit of extra money out of someone, like the way our record deal was set up. It was unheard of to get a record deal like we had. We had so much control. You wouldn't believe just how much control we had. Over everything! The choice of singles. The choice of cover. Who produced us. What the videos looked like. Every aspect was under our control.

Stuart now recalls another special time in between the release of the debut album and the recording of the second.

I remember being at the Ivy Bush in Cwmaman, our local pub at the time. The three of us went out. We thought we'd go and get pissed. We went to the Ivy Bush and there was a band in there playing. They asked us to come on stage and play a song. So we agreed. We played 'A Thousand Trees'. But then we did 'The Bartender and the Thief'. But we'd only just recorded it that day, so nobody had heard it before. So we just said 'We're gonna play you a new song, off the new album. It'll be out in a couple of months time.' So that's the first time anyone had ever heard 'The Bartender and the Thief'. It became our biggest hit, but it was premiered at the Ivy Bush in Cwmaman. So there you are. How amazing's that?'

6

PERFORMANCE AND COCKTAILS

Anyone who says that they're just in it purely for the music is kidding . . . You want to be like the Beatles. Like the Stones. Like Led Zeppelin. You want to sell a million albums! You want to play to 100,000 people in a huge stadium in every city you go to.

Stuart Cable, November 2007

NOVEMBER 2007, THE RED DRAGON CENTRE, CARDIFF

Performance and Cocktails was the record that propelled the Stereophonics into the big time. The debut album, *Word Gets Around*, had sold well. It was an amazing first step onto the ladder. It got the threesome noticed by the British public. As a result, the Stereophonics were now a name. But their follow-up album was to take them even further. I've arranged to meet Stuart at Xfm South Wales in Cardiff to find out about the next step on his journey to rock success. Stuart presents two radio shows: one for Kerrang radio, owned by the famous UK magazine of the same name, the other for the indie/rock station Xfm. This radio station recently won a licence to broadcast to south Wales. There are also Xfms for London, Manchester and Glasgow. It's a popular radio franchise. Xfm's new studios are based in Cardiff Bay, inside the offices of Red Dragon Radio (both stations are owned by London-based radio group GCAP). The old Atlantic Wharf cinema and entertainment complex in the Bay has recently been renamed after the radio station. It's now the Red Dragon Centre. It has a nightclub, a cinema, a bowling alley, a pub, an exhibition based around the TV series *Dr Who* and a number of restaurants and cafe bars.

I walk through the centre, heading towards Red Dragon Radio's reception. Inside, the radio station is very modern and impressive. Even now, at the weekend, around twenty news, presenting and production staff are at work in the centre of the office. The walls at the top and far right of the room are lined with radio studios. Inside one of these, Stuart has just finished his show for Xfm. The red light flicks off. The show is now off the air. I push open the heavy, sound-proofed door and step inside.

'Alright, Jeff,' says Stuart. 'How you doing?' The show, it seems, has been a good one.

This radio station may have only just launched, but it has spent a fortune on a big publicity campaign across south Wales. The presenters of Xfm have been plastered on posters across the region in cartoon form, drawn to look like members of the Marvel comic *The X-Men*. Stuart has been drawn sitting behind a drum set in a lycra X-Man outfit, banging away at the drums with his hair on fire. Stuart presents two shows over the weekend. If he's away touring, he'll pre-record them.

He hasn't done many shows for the station yet, but he's loving it so far. 'Of course you're loving it,' I tell him. 'You're basically being paid to play your favourite songs!'

'Yeah!' he laughs, thinking about it. 'You're right. It's flipping fantastic.' He laughs again as he thinks about what a great gig this radio presenting lark is. I myself present a rock show on Sunshine Radio in Herefordshire and Monmouthshire. It's one of the most enjoyable jobs I've ever had, given my love of rock music. We chat about our respective roles.

> The people from Xfm will let me play anything – even 'By-Tor and the Snow Dog' by Rush, or 'Achilles Last Stand' by Led Zeppelin. I can play those ten-minute songs. My shows are more about the music than myself. I keep the chat very short. I'll play songs back-to-back, then I'll do a quick link about my memories of playing with those people. The listeners just want to hear some good rock music. I also like the fact that Xfm take my opinions on board. But it's great to be able to play all the songs that I loved growing up, and not the obvious songs like 'Paranoid' or 'Stairway to Heaven', but the more obscure stuff.

Stuart decides we should grab a cup of tea from the cafe inside the main area of the Red Dragon Centre, next to the cinema. After finding a seat, and being served, we both sit down with our drinks and I ask Stuart about *Performance and Cocktails*. Just how big a record was this for the Stereophonics?

Performance and Cocktails

Performance and Cocktails was released in March 1999. It entered the UK album charts at number one. Overall, the album spawned five hit singles, including 'The Bartender and the Thief', 'Just Looking', 'Pick a Part That's New', 'Hurry Up and Wait' and 'I Wouldn't Believe Your Radio'.

'That was a massive record,' he says. 'Absolutely massive!'

That was probably the record that put us into Wembley Arena, the Birmingham NEC and the Manchester Evening News Arena. Just as important was the first single: 'The Bartender and the Thief'. I remember sitting in the studio – it was Peter Gabriel's studio, Real World. We were coming towards the end of the session. We'd recorded, I think, nearly all of the songs for the album. It was either a Saturday morning, or Sunday morning. It was quite a nice day, and I remember Kelly coming in and playing me the riff to 'Bartender.'

Oblivious to the passing members of the public heading to the cinema, or bowling alley, Stuart now starts playing air guitar and singing the opening riff to the song.

Dow dow-dow dow dow-dow dow. I was blown away when I heard it. I was like 'What's that, man!' And Kelly said 'I don't know. I just started playing it.' So I told him we should record it straight away. I also told Kelly that the song should have a really kind of trashy start. So I banged out this opening section. I was whacking the cymbals and Kelly was grinding out the riff. We just sat there, knowing this song was incredible. Then Kelly went away to write some lyrics and later we phoned our manager John Brand and got him to come to the studio to listen to the song.

We then spent that day, and that night, recording it. Kelly wrote these great, quirky words, about the bartender and the thief, which was very apt for the music in a strange way. And we kind of thought, 'Damn it! Let's release it as a single.' Even though it was the least commercial thing we'd ever done. We thought Radio 1 would hate it. But they weren't playing us anyway. Because if you remember, back in those days, around 1998, Radio 1 was king. If you got A-listed by them, on day-time radio, then you went through the roof in terms of record sales. But we were getting quite pissed off with Radio 1 at the time. What had happened was, on our first album, Radio 1 was saying 'Oh yeah. We'll support you on the next single, "A Thousand Trees"! We love "A Thousand Trees"! We're gonna support you all the way.' But they never did. Then it was going to be 'Traffic'. 'Yeah, yeah,' they'd enthuse. 'We love "Traffic". Great song. We'll support you all the way on "Traffic".' But again, they never did. We just got so disillusioned with them. 'Bartender' was the least commercial song we'd recorded. We loved it and we thought that Radio 1 would hate it. But who cares as they weren't playing our songs anyway. Then all of a sudden, 'Bartender' got A-listed by Radio 1 – they played it day and night – and it shot to number three in the UK charts. We were all sitting there going 'Bloody hell, this is weird. A rock song doing that well.' So that record is probably one of the biggest, if not the biggest, in the career of Stereophonics.

The Stereophonics were starting to flex their muscles in the recording studio as well. Their record deal gave them an amazing amount of control. Heaven help anyone who interfered!

'We actually fired our A&R man (Artists and Repertory) because he was meddling,' Stuart informs me.

He came down to our studio when we were recording *Performance and Cocktails*. Now, do you remember, at the time when we were laying down *Performance and Cocktails*, everyone else was putting a brass section on their records? Everyone! And this guy kept telling us that we had to put brass on our new record. Well, that was like a red rag to a bull. Me and Kelly looked at each other and both agreed that we were not putting any brass on the record. So, we went outside, phoned John, our manager, and told him that we were going to ban this man from our studio. John was unsure. But Kelly said 'We've got to. The man's an idiot. He wants strings on this. Brass on that. But that's not the band we are.' Subsequently, he got taken off us, and a few months later he was sacked. But I don't feel bad about it because I always say that some people should sell carpets, and some people should be in the music business. Unfortunately, he was a carpet salesman! He didn't belong in the music business. He didn't know what the Stereophonics were about. He wanted to put brass on our records, just because all his mates, at other record companies, were saying 'Brass is the way forward. You got to put brass on all your records.' Instead, he should have been looking at the individual package, and asking himself, 'Well, does it suit them? How will they replicate it live?' He wanted it, just because it was the in thing at the time and he gave no thought for us. So we told him where to go! It wasn't going to happen. Most bands would have been beaten into a corner and told to do it. But we had a great contract. We had 100 per cent artistic control. We told the record company how our records would sound, how the videos would look, what the photographs should look like, what songs went on the albums, what singles were released . . . everything! Obviously, we also worked with the record company and their experience – we'd be fools not to. But, if there was something we thought was really, really bad, we would, and could, say no. I don't think anyone will get a record deal like that again!

In that answer, Stuart mentions the band's videos. For *Performance and Cocktails*, the band made more and more exotic and elaborate videos to accompany their singles. For the first single, 'The Bartender and the Thief', the band ended up in Thailand. On the River Kwai, of all places.

Yeah. The River Kwai. That was cool. We flew there, and did an acoustic show at a music shop somewhere, and then spent the next two days on the River Kwai shooting this video. The video was based on the film *Apocalypse Now*.

The video opens with the three members of the Stereophonics travelling down the river on an army boat. As they arrive dockside, fireworks explode, and the band take to a floating platform to perform the song to the troops. Stuart plays the drums throughout wearing a metal US army helmet.

Those guys you see in the video are real Thai army guys. 'We got all of them for £15 a day. [He chuckles.] Not individually. But £15 for the whole lot. About 200 people. They built that platform we sang on, and a watchtower for authenticity. We spent two days on the River Kwai. We did a photo shoot for the front cover of *Kerrang* magazine there as well. It was so warm and such a cheap place, but we didn't have a lot of time to look around.

We would do the video shoot for most of the day and then get back to the hotel to crash out. Before you knew it, it was time to get back to the video shoot again. But we had some good fun doing videos for that album. We had the one for the song 'Pick a Part That's New', which was a spoof of the classic film *The Italian Job*. It was good, because we went to Turin to do that video. The place where they actually filmed *The Italian Job*. Pretty cool city Turin.

'Pick a Part' closely followed the plot of *The Italian Job*. The band start out loading gold from a heist into three Minis – one red, one white and one blue, just like in the Michael Caine film. The locations were the same ones used in the film. When not racing around in Minis, the band were filmed playing their instruments inside an old coach, supposedly hanging off the edge of a cliff, just as in the film's famous final scene.

Stuart enjoyed making that video. Boys will be boys.

'Hurry Up and Wait' was based on *M*A*S*H*. We went to Sydney to film that one. The video for 'Just Looking' was done in Scotland. It's the video where I'm in a Jaguar car with Kelly. I'm driving and the car goes off the road into the water. Kelly gets out, but I've got to stay in the car as it sinks. I'm the last one out. Just! That wasn't based on a film, or anything. That was probably one of Kelly's wild ideas.

So that was just to get you under water in a car, I ask him.

'Yeah, man,' says Stuart excitedly, sensing a chance to start a conspiracy theory. 'He was trying to kill me. He could have sacked me there and then! That's funny looking back. But on the whole, when we did the videos for the singles from *Performance and Cocktails*, we went to some very exotic locations.'

A second cup of tea is brought to our table. Once it's served, I ask Stuart about another offshoot of the band's new-found success. 'I guess the fact the album sold so well saw you, as a band, playing bigger and bigger venues?'

Oh, yeah. Massively so. We went from playing to 400 people a night to playing Wembley Arena, which was 12,000, and the Manchester Evening News Arena, which holds 18,000. Then you start doing consecutive nights. You just sit there and think 'Wow – how big is this!' And then you get people like Jimmy Page and Robert Plant from Led Zeppelin turning up. As the band got bigger, and hotter, these things started happening. But the single, 'The Bartender and the Thief', was one of the main reasons it happened really.

Performance and Cocktails saw another landmark for the band. They won a major award for it: the Kerrang Magazine Award for Best Album. They band beat off the likes of Marilyn Manson, System of a Down, Red Hot Chili Peppers and Silverchair.

'Yeah, we did man.' Stuart is still immensely proud of this award, even nine years on.

We couldn't believe it. We knew we'd won, though. We were told by our record company that we'd done it. It made up for the fact that we just totally got shoved out of the Brit Awards earlier that year. We'd outsold

Travis by 600,000 copies, yet they won Best Band, Best Album, Best everything! At the time, to win a Brit Award meant a lot of things. One of those things is that you can sell a million copies off the back of that award.

Everyone gets into this game to be the biggest band they can. Anyone who says that they're just in it purely for the music is kidding. No, they're not. You want to be like the Beatles. Like the Stones. Like Led Zeppelin. You want to sell a million albums! You want to play to 100,000 people in a huge stadium in every city you go to. So we were disappointed to lose that Brit Award. We won one later on, though. That was an award voted for by the public. I always say that the Brit Award we finally did win means a lot to me. I've got it on my mantelpiece at home. It means a lot because of the simple fact that it was voted for by the fans at home. And that was the last year they allowed voting because, if you remember, Supergrass won it, Blur won it, Oasis won it and then the Stereophonics won it. It was all rock acts. So the record companies wanted a slice of the action for their boy bands and girl bands. So they scrapped it to stop the public voting.

For 1999's Kerrang Award the band had another surprise. The award was presented to them by TV legend David Soul – best known as the 1970s detective Ken Hutchinson in *Starsky and Hutch*. A total legend, Soul was met by a massively loud and warm greeting from the audience at the ceremony. He passed the trophy to the Stereophonics, as Stuart burst into a quick verse of 'Silver Lady' – the actor's big hit single from the 1970s. Stuart thinks back to that moment on stage with a TV legend, and the decision to sing his famous ballad to him.

'I don't know whether he liked it, or whether he wanted to punch me in the face.' Stuart breaks into 'Silver Lady' again. He obviously secretly loves it. He knows all the words!

I think, I was a bit drunk actually. I did sing 'Silver Lady', but he was cool, man. He said he'd moved to London and was now living there. Then we got our picture taken with him and the presenter Tommy Vance came in to congratulate us. That was pretty cool, because he is the godfather of rock. His rock show on Radio 1 was the best!

But to beat Marilyn Manson and Silverchair – who were hot at that time as well – that was great. It led to us headlining the Reading and Leeds music festivals. That was mental. The Reading bill was probably the most diverse bill ever. There was Slipknot, then Rage Against The Machine and then us as headliners. Obviously, they approached our management and we spoke about it for a few months. When they came back and told us the support acts – Richard and myself are big Rage Against The Machine fans – we were like 'Bloody hell. How do we follow that, man!' But you know, you have to realize that when you are a headlining band, most of the people in the crowd have bought tickets to see you. So it was a pleasure. And Tom Jones came on and did 'Mama Told Me Not To Come' with us, just to top the whole thing off. That was pretty special doing that song live with him.

Performance and Cocktails

The Stereophonics collaborated with Welsh legend Tom Jones on a cover version of the Randy Newman song 'Mama Told Me Not To Come'. The song was for his hit album *Reload*, which sold six million copies worldwide. It made number one in the UK in both 1999 and 2000.

Performance and Cocktails was the Stereophonics's high point. It was the last time the band wrote an album together. The fractures would start to appear on the recording of the group's next album *Just Enough Education to Perform*, or *J.E.E.P.* as it became known. The third album was to be the beginning of the end of Stuart's time with the Stereophonics.

7

JUST ENOUGH EDUCATION
TO PERFORM

I simply had a CD sent to me through the post with the songs on. There was a letter as well from Kelly saying that he didn't want to play big anthemic songs anymore . . . I thought to myself, 'Ok yeah. That's fine. But then again if it ain't broke – don't fix it.'

Stuart Cable, Cardiff, 2007

In 2001, the Stereophonics's third album was originally to be called *JEEP*. Car manufacturer Daimler-Chrysler, though, had other ideas. They'd copyrighted this name and didn't want some UK rock band using it, so it was changed to *Just Enough Education to Perform*, more often than not shortened to *J.E.E.P.*

The first two Stereophonics albums had been written together by the band at the community centre in Cwmaman. Kelly Jones had written most of the material, but the other two members chipped in with their ideas. This meant the songs altered, evolving as they were given 'the Stereophonics treatment'.

I'm sitting with Stuart Cable drinking tea in Cardiff Bay. We're in an entertainment complex named after the local radio station based here, the Red Dragon Centre. It's midday and just behind us, the queue is starting to grow at the nearby cinema complex, as the first showing of today's films is just minutes away.

A number of people walking to the cinema notice Stuart, nudge their friends and point. 'Look, is that the drummer from the Stereophonics?' whispers one man to his mate. Another simply shouts a friendly greeting. 'Alright, Stuart mate!'

Stuart is used to all this attention. He's a popular figure, particularly in Wales. He waves back with a big smile. 'I'm fine, man,' he shouts back in reply.

Our conversation turns to the Stereophonics's third album. This record saw a major change in the way the band operated. Stuart shakes his head, as he pours a little more milk into his tea, while remembering the way the album was done.

'*J.E.E.P.* was all written in Kelly's house!' It's the first time this morning that the smile has left Stuart's face.

> That was the album when he started writing separately – away from us. I simply had a CD sent to me through the post with the songs on. There was a letter as well from Kelly saying that he didn't want to play big anthemic songs anymore. Songs like 'Just Looking' and 'The Bartender and the Thief'. He didn't want to do that style of music any more. I thought to myself, 'Ok yeah. That's fine. But then again if it ain't broke – don't fix it.'

When it was released, the album was panned by the critics, the same critics who'd lapped up the sound on the band's first two albums. I hesitate before mentioning the reviews to Stuart. How much had those reviews hurt him upon the album's release? Maybe he has thicker skin than most musicians. I take a deep breath, and ask him what the band thought of the primarily bad reviews of *J.E.E.P.*?

One review in the magazine *Kerrang* – usually a staunch Stereophonics supporter – was particularly cruel. I remind Stuart how the magazine wrote: 'You might like to know that if *Just Enough Education to Perform*, the third album from the Stereophonics, were a debut album from an unknown band, then *Kerrang* probably wouldn't touch it with a bucketful of disinfectant and a cattle prod.' The review bemoaned the lack of 'high energy anthems, football stand choruses and occasional AC/DC references that permeated the band's previous two albums'.

Kerrang called it 'Not only a dog of an album, but an awfully slow one at that.' Stuart winces at the recollection of that review from a supposed supporter of the band.

> To be honest, there was not a lot we could do then, because the band was more or less being run as Kelly's group. Kelly would take the brunt of the flak, and to be honest, he would take it as a personal insult. I would sit there and say to him, 'Look. It's just one person's opinion. At the end of the day, you can only please some of the people some of the time, and not all of the people all of the time. You just can't do it.' I mean, yes, we made a great debut album. Yes, we made a flipping fantastic second album. But on the third record, unfortunately, the wheels fell off a bit. Whose fault was that? I don't know. Could it be the fact Kelly wanted to write it on his own?

Could it be that we lost the energy we had when working together in a room in Cwmaman? Some might say yes. Some might say no. I don't know! I think there are some great songs on that album, but it went in an acoustic direction far too quickly. There were some great rock songs on there, but not in the same league as the three-minute 'in-your-face' tracks like 'A Thousand Trees' and 'More Life in a Tramp's Vest'. The album missed the big choruses.

We chose to release something like 'Step On My Old Size Nines' as a single, which was very much in the same vein as 'Traffic'. Now 'Traffic' was a big song for us – a big live song as well. That second verse, just after the solo with the line 'She waits tables . . .' Well, bloody hell. At every concert we played in the UK, Kelly would stop singing there, because it was pointless. The crowd would sing it back to us so loud. And they did the same for 'Step On My Old Size Nines' as well. But I can see it from a journalist's point of view, where you can easily say that the wheels were coming off. Who knows. You can only work with what's in front of you. Kelly wrote the album himself. If one person makes it difficult for other people, sometimes you just have to go along with it.

I did an interview the other day. It was with an Irish guy, who runs a website called *Word Gets Around*, which is self-explanatory. He's been pestering me for a long time to do this interview. During it, he was saying to me how much he loved the first two albums, but how he's felt less strongly about every subsequent one. He's right! Everybody that comes on to me, they still just talk about *Word Gets Around* and *Performance and Cocktails*.

Still, *Just Enough Education to Perform* was another number one album and sold more than two and a half million records. The band also moved up another notch in the live area playing to bigger and bigger audiences. One of the main reason for this was the hit single 'Handbags and Gladrags'. Stuart smiles again.

Now moving on very quickly – while it stays in my mind – that was the song that made the *J.E.E.P.* album really sell. We recorded that song for a B-side, as a laugh, in Jools Holland's studio. That was about six months after the album was released. But David Steel, who was head of V2 Records at the time, heard the song and said he wanted to release it as a single. We were like 'We don't really know if we want to do that.' But finally we agreed. We told him that we'd prefer it if they repackaged the album to include 'Handbags and Gladrags'. We'd already sold about 800,000 copies of *J.E.E.P.* and then we sold another million or so, off the back of just that one tune. Just off 'Handbags and Gladrags'. So really, from a marketing point of view, it was a great call from a guy who's head of a record company and doing his job very well. It was a cover, but it did very well and kept us playing the big stadiums.

'Handbags and Gladrags' was written in 1967 by Mike d'Abo. Chris Farlowe recorded it first in that year and Rod Stewart recorded it two years later, releasing it as a single in 1972. Neither version made the top forty in either the UK or US. As neither single was a hit, I tell Stuart how a lot of people still don't realize that their version of the song was a cover. Some people think it was a Stereophonics original. Stuart agrees.

This journalist from Ireland phoned me once and asked 'Was it Kelly who wrote "Handbags and Gladrags"?' This guy's only twenty or twenty-one. And I said to him 'Well, it was written by Mike d'Abo.' He was baffled and asked 'Right! Er! Who's Mike d'Abo?' So I told him that Mike was the singer from Manfred Mann. I told him that 'Handbags and Gladrags' was a big Rod Stewart song. Others have done it as well though, including Chris Farlowe, who obviously did it first. The story was that Rod Stewart actually wanted it first, but apparently he didn't have a singles deal at the time. Just an album deal. So the song wasn't released for a while. It was only available as a track on his album, *An Old Raincoat Won't Let You Down*. It took another three years for it to be issued as a single.

But it's funny you know, Mike d'Abo turned up at a show when we played the Birmingham National Indoor Arena. He came backstage, and he said to Kelly and me, 'I've got loads of songs I've written, which you're welcome to use.' We laughed and I said 'Yeah! No wonder. We've just sold a million copies for you. I bet you can't wait to throw more songs our way.' He was a nice guy. I bet us doing his song was his biggest payday for years. But that's the way it goes.

I ask Stuart how the band came to cover that song, particularly as it doesn't come across as a typical Stereophonics song.

Well, we went to New York to mix *J.E.E.P.* and we spent three weeks there. We rented a three-bed flat in Soho. While we were there, every morning, Richard Jones would play the Rod Stewart album which had this song on it. And Kelly said to me, 'Why don't we do a cover of it? It'll be something people won't expect us to do.' And he had something there. You can hear the vocal line is very, very good for Kelly's voice. A lot of people say he sounds like an early Rod Stewart anyway. So we went back to the UK and started jamming to it. Then we had the opportunity to use Jools Holland's studio. The song did eventually get released as a single, as well as being added to the repacked album. We recorded the video for it in the Roundhouse in London with an orchestra, and it was done in two takes. We ran through it once and recorded that one. Then we ran through it again for luck. And I think it's the first take that you see. But, yeah, that was a big tune for us.

J.E.E.P.

The first two singles from *Just Enough Education to Perform* were 'Mr Writer' and 'Have a Nice Day'. They both made number five in the UK singles chart. 'Have a Nice Day' would become one of the band's most popular songs. It was also used in the 2004 remake of the film *Dawn of the Dead*.

We order another cup of tea and I ask Stuart about another song from the album: the controversial 'Mr Writer'. It was written about a music journalist who went on the road with the band and then thoroughly slagged them off in print. Kelly Jones was not pleased and immortalized the journalist in song.

'Ahh, yeah. Dirty blighter!' He chuckles but I get the impression he's not taking this spat too seriously.

It was either a guy from *Q Magazine*, or something similar. He came on the road with us in America. He was a nice guy. Really cool and so friendly with us. But he went back and basically wrote a load of shit about us. I'm sure we all took offence at the time. But Kelly's the man with the pen. And he was furious. In all fairness, I did say when he wrote it 'Are you sure you want to do this?' I felt he was targeting every music journalist, not just one – and, lo and behold, he upset a lot of people. A hell of a lot of people. Some quite influential people as well. I don't know if that was the nail in Kelly's coffin, because the interviews seemed to fall off after that. They just dried up. You no longer see the Stereophonics in *Mojo*, or *Q Magazine*. The big features seem to have gone. I really don't know. Kelly seemed to be biting the hand that feeds. But he wrote it. We recorded it. Whether it was a good thing I don't know.

Whilst all was not well in the Stereophonics camp, there were elements of the *Just Enough Education to Perform* period that Stuart really enjoyed, especially the big double-header concerts at Donnington and the Millennium Stadium in Cardiff.

That was fun. That was called 'The Day at the Races'. Initially, one of the gigs was supposed to be at Chepstow racetrack, with the other at Donnington. But obviously we had to call off the Chepstow gig, because of an outbreak of foot and mouth disease in the UK. So we ended up in the Millennium Stadium in Cardiff instead, which was fantastic. We had The Black Crowes play there with us. We love that band. So those things were great. The Donnington thing was also great, because I'd been there to see the Monsters Of Rock Festival in 1987. So to be on that stage, and see 50,000 people in front of you, was pretty cool, really.

Looking back at the *J.E.E.P.* album, there were some good songs. Kelly wrote tracks like 'Vegas Two Times', which sounds very much like The Black Crowes. Some of it was also very heavily influenced by Neil Young. I love Neil Young. 'Step On My Old Size Nines' is a good song. I also liked a track called 'Rooftop'. I enjoyed playing that one live. But overall as an album, it was the record where the band started to fragment. It just wasn't the same.

Also relationships into the band started to change. This was the album where Kelly decided – without telling me and Richard – to change the royalty splits. It had been divided between the three of us as 50 per cent for Kelly and 25 per cent each for me and Richard. He altered that to 70 per cent for him and 15 per cent for me and 15 per cent for Rich. That wasn't helpful.

There were other problems too. My wife at the time was pregnant, so I was going back and forth to Wales from Real World Studios in Bath, where it was being recorded. Kelly was always asking me to stay behind to do more drum tracks, or to top them up. I'd wonder why he was asking me this, so I'd speak to the producer, Marshall Bird, to find out what the problem was. He'd say 'Nah. Kelly's wrong. You don't need to redo the drums at all. That's simply not the case.' So I'm trying to get on with my life. Me and my wife are expecting a baby at any time. That was quite stressful. But all Kelly's worried about is the album. I mean, yeah, granted everyone's got to be focused on it. But Kelly couldn't see the fact that someone had got something else on their plate. So that became a very difficult record.

It was also the first time Stuart thought about leaving the band, the band containing his two best friends. They'd fought their way to the top, but now it was in danger of coming off the rails. The tour to promote the album was no easier for Stuart than the making of the record.

After that record was made, and we stared touring, that was the time when I first thought about quitting, really. But to be honest with you – and I'll put my hand on my heart – the reason why I didn't leave the band there and then was because I wasn't financially secure enough. If I had been, I'd have quit right then. I wasn't happy with the way Kelly changed the royalty split. He didn't even speak to me and Richard about it. He got the management to do it for him. I had an e-mail from our manager, John Brand, and then a telephone conversation with him, and he said 'Stuart, this is what Kelly wants to do. End of story.' I couldn't believe that we'd been friends all these years and he didn't even come to tell me in person about the changes that affected the whole of the band. So that was a big nail in the coffin for me. Then it just escalated from there. When my wife and me had a child, I used to spend a lot of time with our new baby. You have duties as a dad. But Kelly was always having a go at me about it. He just didn't get it. When you have a child, your priorities change. I can't stay up every night drinking and partying. You know, when I went home, I had to become a father. I had to do all those family type of things. Since then, Kelly's also become a father. I think now he understands, but back then he didn't get it. He saw me as being difficult, simply because I'd become a family man. So that was around the time I first started thinking about leaving the band.

So the seeds were being sown. The Stereophonics was Stuart's way of life. It was more than just being in a band. Kelly and Richard had been close friends of his since childhood. Worse was to come for the drummer when the band assembled to make its fourth album. But on the way, Stuart Cable got to see the highlife as the Stereophonics soared higher and higher. He travelled to wonderful and exotic places and met some of his musical heroes.

8

'HAVE A NICE DAY'

The [Rolling Stones] are like little children really. Albeit very old, little children. We were playing snooker with Keith and Ronnie . . . they started arguing like two kids . . . Me and Kelly were just standing there with our snooker cues saying 'Hey boys, it's your shot.'

Stuart Cable, Cardiff, 2007

28 JUNE 1999, LONDON, CAFÉ DE PARIS

The Stereophonics are standing in the middle of London's famous Café de Paris. This evening is a benefit gig set up to help two charities linked to Led Zeppelin guitarist Jimmy Page: S.C.R.E.A.M. (Supporting Children through Re-education And Music) and The ABC (Action for Brazil's Children) Trust.

Four hundred people will be at this invitation-only event with the likes of Alice Cooper, Roger Taylor from Queen and tennis stars Pat Cash and John McEnroe in the audience. The event is sponsored by Calvin Klein, who invited almost all of the guests. Thousands of fans crowded outside the club for hours in the hope of getting an earful of the excitement happening inside.

The Stereophonics had heard about the show and managed to get on the bill. They got a message to Jimmy Page saying 'We'd love to come and play.' Page had dropped in to see the band live at one of their gigs before and likes the Welsh trio. So he was happy to have them on board.

Now the gig's here and the Stereophonics are star-struck. 'Look,' says Stuart excitedly. 'That's flippin' Steven Tyler. In fact, it's all of Aerosmith.' Nearby are the Black Crowes and – sharp intake of breath – Jimmy Page himself.

Stuart looks around, spots another of his heroes and taps Kelly on the shoulder. 'Look man! It's Billy Duffy from The Cult.' Richard and Kelly are too timid, and too star-struck, to go up and say hello to the guitarist. So, the more outgoing and ebullient Cable is left to make the introductions.

'Alright, Billy! I'm Stuart Cable, from the Stereophonics. We love your band, man. It's mad meeting you. We used to play your stuff, when we were a covers band starting out.'

Billy looks at Stuart with a smile. 'No way. What did you used to play?'

Stuart thinks back to his former life with Zephyr in Cwmaman many, many moons ago. 'Well, we loved doing "Little Devil" and "Wild Flower". Those absolutely rock!'

Billy is taken aback and, in true rock 'n' roll style, replies 'Fuck off. Did you really? Rockin'! Do you want to play it tonight?'

Stuart is dumbfounded, but quickly composes himself. 'Yeah, I'd love to, but we'd better check with Kelly, because he's the singer.' A quick word later and Kelly has agreed. He'd love to do it. 'OK. Let's play!' says Duffy and he and Stuart walk to the bar to write out the lyrics for Kelly.

Later, at the end of the Sterophonics set, Kelly Jones announces to the select crowd, 'We've got a special guest with us tonight. He wants to play with us. I think you're gonna love this. Please welcome – from The Cult – Billy Duffy!'

The guitarist strides on, as cool as hell, in black T-shirt and black leathers. He doesn't have a guitar with him as he hadn't expected to play tonight. So he puts on Kelly's guitar. It fits like a banjo! Kelly's strap is too high. Billy Duffy's trying to lower it, but it's not easy.

Eventually, the Cult's axeman puts his foot on the monitor and cranks out the raucous opening riff to 'Wild Flower', from the band's tremendous *Electric* album. He turns to Stuart and fixes him with a friendly stare. Time for the drums! Stuart, beaming from ear to ear, starts pounding out the heavy riff. It's one of those rock 'n' roll moments!

NOVEMBER 2007, THE RED DRAGON CENTRE, CARDIFF

Back at the coffee shop in Cardiff Bay nearly eight years later, and Stuart Cable is staring into space as he retells the tale of that wonderful night when the Stereophonics played with Billy Duffy at Jimmy Page's charity do.

'Jeff, it was great,' he says simply to me. 'We nailed that song. It was bizarre that night. Who'd have thought we'd play "Wild Flower" with Billy Duffy! Crazy. So yeah, when you think back, a lot of great things happened in a very short space of time. Particularly for meeting heroes and that kind of stuff.'

The Stereophonics's, growing success brought them into close quarters with many of their heroes, The Black Crowes for one.

They were great. They taught us a lot. The American ethic of being in a band means that if another band turns up at one of your shows, then they have to play a song with you. They just have to! It's the done thing. I remember we turned up in Japan and The Crowes were playing there in Tokyo that night. So we phoned their tour manager and asked if we could come down. He agreed, so we went down and into their dressing room. We hadn't seen them for a few months. The last time we'd bumped into them was in the States.

So their singer, Chris Robinson, comes up to me and Kelly and says 'Hey, our drummer Steve Gorman told me that you guys used to play our song "Twice As Hard". Do you want to play it tonight? Come on! Stuart can get on the drums. Kelly, you can play guitars. You can sing a verse and then I'll sing a verse.'

I looked at Kelly. He looked at me and we both thought 'Wow'. But that's the way it was with The Black Crowes. If you turned up at one of their gigs then you had to play. That just didn't happen at our gigs, though. I mean, can you imagine Jimmy Page coming on stage and playing with us? So there we were standing on the side of the stage. There were 3,000 people at this gig in Tokyo. I've never been so nervous in all my life. So Gorman gets up and gives me his drumsticks and his seat. Then he sits there, right behind me, where his drum tech sits. Chris Robinson turns round, and before I know it, he's started the song 'Twice As Hard'. And he's looking at me. I'm thinking 'Jeez, these are people I used to look up to! And now I'm sitting here playing one of their massive hits on stage with them.' That experience was so great – one of my best nights. We get on great with The Black Crowes. They are lovely, lovely people. Did you know that Chris Robinson's father used to come to Ebbw Vale in Wales a lot, because he's a rugby player and ran a rugby team in Atlanta? He used to say to us that he always had guys visiting his house in America from Wales with typical rugby injuries: a nose spread over here and eyes battered to black. Every time we'd see them, he'd say – in a poor impression of a Welsh accent – 'Hey, have you got a bucket of coal for me, man!'

We went to Chris Robinson's place in New York, when he was with Kate Hudson, before they had a kid and got married. We were mixing in New York, went round and played Vegas Two Times for him. And I remember sitting in his living room while he was rolling a joint. He looked at Kelly with his short hair and said 'Hey man, you gotta have long hair to play rock 'n' roll!'

'Have a Nice Day'

The Black Crowes were kicked off a prestigious support slot touring US stadiums with ZZ Top in 1991. The tour was sponsored by Miller Beer, but the band were fired when singer Chris Robinson made a sarcastic comment about commercialism on stage. He told the audience that The Crowes played live rock 'n' roll, as opposed to just doing 'commercials' for their product. A clear dig at ZZ Top! The Black Crowes were bumped from the tour when the singer refused to tone down his comments so as not to upset the sponsor and the headliners.

Stuart laughs at that memory. 'Chris was a good guy. He used to make sure that if we were in the same city he'd drop by and we'd hang out.'

I asked Stuart if he'd played with many more of his musical heroes in his time with the band.

Oh man yes! Just a bit! Obviously, we played some shows with The Who. There was also U2. Growing up, I wasn't a massive U2 fan, but you're so aware they are there and of the massive influence they have in the world of music. And when you see their live show – it's pretty special. That was the Elevation tour in 2001.

Aerosmith was another. That was cool. We did a couple of shows with Aerosmith and they were quite funny. I got into a big conversation with their lead singer Steven Tyler about the late AC/DC singer Bon Scott, actually. They'd shared a tour bus back in 1976. That was bizarre. It was in Holland, I think he said. But Tyler couldn't remember the year. He'd done too many drugs. Backstage we had a dressing room, then The Black Crowes's dressing room was a little further down and at the end, Aerosmith had this warm-up area. Me and Kelly were talking to Steve Tyler, after which he went into his warm-up room and put AC/DC's *Highway to Hell* on. He was singing along to it and he called us in the room. He started talking about how special Bon was and how he'd forgotten how good a singer he was. So we asked if there was any chance we could stand on the side of the stage that night to watch the show. He said that he'd be delighted for us to be there. So he told us to wait outside our dressing room when we were ready to go on with them. Sure enough their security guy came and got us, and we went up with the band to the side of the stage.

Aerosmith had a big curtain, so they couldn't see the crowd before the show started. Then the intro music starts up, Steven Tyler turns to me and Kelly and says 'This one's for Bon!' Then bang – the curtain goes down and he went on and sang 'Eat the Rich'. We were just standing there blown away.

The Stereophonics also had the privilege to tour with the Rolling Stones, something Stuart won't ever forget.

I love Ronnie Wood. He's great. He's hilarious. He came to watch us when we played Dublin Castle. He's a big snooker fan and, that night, Wales's Mark Williams was in the final with Ken Doherty in the World Snooker Finals. I remember coming off stage, and me and Ronnie just watching the game on the television after the gig. I think we had a bet. A tenner. Obviously I wanted Mark to win. Later that night, we ended up in a pub with Ronnie, before going back to his house and sleeping there. He's an extraordinary guy. He does all these great paintings. They are out of this world. When we woke up in the morning, he was sitting there, reading the *Racing Post* with his glasses on the end of his nose. Coffee in his hand, he said to us 'My driver will give you a lift back into town when you want to go.'

And then from us knowing Ronnie, we did the Rolling Stones tour. The Stones tour was great. They're like little children really. Albeit very old, little children. We were playing snooker with Keith and Ronnie. During the game Keith bought in this semi-acoustic Gibson guitar worth probably a hundred thousand pounds. Keith's probably had it since day one in 1952. Ronnie asked him if he could use it on stage that night. Keith said no. Ronnie asked why. Keith asked what would happen if he fell over and broke the neck off. Then they started arguing like two kids. About this guitar. Me and Kelly were just standing there with our snooker cues saying 'Hey boys, it's your shot.' And then Charlie Watts just comes in and stands there. He just watched them with a resigned smile. He'd seen this millions of times before. Good fun though and we had a great laugh. The Stones were very nice to us.

At the height of our success, we did some great things, went to some brilliant places and met some amazing people. Through our music, we were given a great opportunity to experience some wonderful things. It was a shame that the next record, our fourth, would be the end of it for me.

By the time the Stereophonics went back into the studio in 2002 to record *You Gotta Go There to Come Back*, like a bad marriage the cracks in Stuart and Kelly's relationship were getting bigger. Stuart was getting unhappier with the set-up and the clock was ticking on his time with the band.

9

YOU'VE GOTTA GO THERE TO COME BACK

> Kelly just phoned me up from New York. He simply said, 'That's it! You're out of the band! But I was like 'Alright. Cool!' . . . I told him that he'd known I was planning to leave at the end of the year anyway.'
>
> Stuart Cable, Cardiff, 2007

The Stereophonics's fourth album, *You've Gotta Go There to Come Back*, was released in June 2003. Not long after, Stuart Cable would become an ex-Stereophonic.

Soon after the album's release, Stuart had flown out to San Francisco for the US leg of the band's tour. The drummer arrived two days after Kelly and Richard had touched down in the States. They'd arrived early to play an acoustic set on radio, a set Stuart wasn't needed for.

You Gotta Go There to Come Back

You Gotta Go There to Come Back from 2003 was the band's fourth album and their third consecutive UK number one. The track 'Maybe Tomorrow' was used in the credits for the Oscar-winning film *Crash*.

'That was handy,' recalls Stuart as we head back to the Red Dragon Radio studios.

> I had an abscess on my bum, and I was in agony. I could barely sit down through the flight, and certainly couldn't play drums. I was in a lot of pain. I went to a doctor and then later I had an operation. Three days of recovering later, the doctor's telling me I'm fit to play. So the band had a meeting in LA.
>
> I said to Kelly and Richard that I could do the remaining shows. But the boys said I should go home and get some rest, because I needed to be fit for the European tour.
>
> I said I'd stay, but they insisted I went home. So I did, and that's when I had the phone call.

Stuart makes little quotation marks with his fingers to indicate that this was no ordinary phone call.

I look startled. 'That's how you found out?' I ask. 'Not face-to-face, but on the phone?'

The drummer nods his head silently to confirm that this is correct.

> Oh yes! Kelly just phoned me up from New York. He simply said, 'That's it! You're out of the band!' But I was like 'Alright. Cool!'
>
> That threw him. He said to me 'Well, what do you mean, cool?' So I told him that he'd known I was planning to leave at the end of the year anyway.
>
> The whole thing was a shambles, because next up they issued a press release without me knowing – which obviously upset me and my family. Kelly has since apologized, but that's no good. The damage had been done. The hurt was caused.

The Stereophonics had sacked Stuart, claiming in a bluntly worded statement on their official website that the drummer and founder member had 'lacked commitment'. It said the decision to let their 'brother' go was 'heartbreaking'.

The statement, penned by Kelly, read:

> Me and Stuart started a band when I was twelve. Emotionally to me this is heartbreaking, I love him like a brother, but commitment-wise there have been issues since *Just Enough Education to Perform*.
>
> We've tried resolving them, but things stayed the same. Myself and Richard miss Stuart already, a band is like a gang and a lot of the time he simply wasn't there, although it was our fault to allow this situation to develop in the first place.

Kelly Jones told the UK press at the time that Stuart's sacking wasn't a bad thing. 'It's not the beginning of the end for us,' he told Cathryn Scott of the *Big Issue* magazine on 1 November 2003.

> The band is stronger than it's ever been. This band has never been so positive. I'm not going to bad mouth Stuart to anyone. He's my oldest friend and we've been through everything together. It's sad, and it's a shame, but being in a band is a massive commitment and there's been a lot of business since our *Just Enough Education to Perform* album. Stuart knows, and I know, that we're not going to make a rash decision on a friend we've known since we were four.

I asked Stuart about these 'commitment' issues mentioned in the website statement and in press interviews at the time. Did his work on radio and TV get in the way of the Stereophonics?

'Absolutely not!' insists Stuart. We stop walking and he turns to face me to make his point.

I don't think I did anything that was wrong. I don't know what the commitment thing was all about. It's not like I was sitting on a beach, refusing to play shows. I always did the TV shows during time off from the band. That had been agreed by the three of us. My TV work never led to any shows being cancelled, nor any videos being cancelled, nor any recording sessions or interviews or whatever!

If Kelly didn't like my radio and TV work then why didn't he tell me? We could have discussed it. That remark in the press release about me missing gigs and rehearsals really did blacken my name. At the end of the day, it'll all come out in the wash. People will find out the truth. I believe that part of the reason I got sacked from the band is that people were into me, more than Kelly. I'm quite a quick-witted guy. I love having a laugh. I love having a big joke. I go on TV shows and give as good as I get. I was the one who used to go nuts at the gigs, pull the funny faces and do the antics like throwing drumsticks into the crowd.

Stuart pauses and takes a deep breath.

Kelly's a great singer, and good-looking boy, like, but I'm a fan of entertaining people. I don't think he liked that – me upstaging him. I think that was part of the problem. But it all goes back to the same old thing though: there's no 'I' in team.

Having played with Kelly and Richard since he was a teenager, Stuart is clearly upset to have lost two of his best friends. It's this loss that makes the end of his time with the Stereophonics so bitter. Stuart's still angry at what happened and how it happened. But it's also clear that he misses his old friends – at least to some degree.

Yes, I am upset at losing such close friends. The whole affair could have been done in a more manly – and a more friendly – fashion. At the end of the day, Kelly knew that I didn't want to be in the band much longer. So why didn't he just say 'Let's sit down and plan what we are going to do! Let's work out how we do this financially, paperwork wise.' But, no. It had to be done the Kelly Jones way. It was all cloak and dagger. There was a lot of taking sides and it didn't need to be that way. I'm a great believer in karma and it will come around and bite you in the arse. It will! It does piss you off, though, when you look back at all the hard work you've put into the band. All the interviews, the hours of travelling around the world, all the great music – just for one person to pull the plug, and really mess it all up.

Another cause of upset for Stuart was the band's tenth anniversary DVD, *Rewind*: the history of the band as told by . . . two-thirds of them!

I'd not spoken to Kelly for about two years and then his name came up on my phone as it rang one day. I answered and he told me about the DVD they'd made about the history of the band. He asked me to watch it and said that if there was anything I didn't like, it could be taken out. So I put the DVD on in the house and it was good to be honest. I enjoyed looking back at the old footage, seeing how stupid we were in those days.

And then I see Kelly and Richard being interviewed about my sacking. Well, I wanted my say on that, plus I wanted to talk about my time in the band. It was the three of us, after all. But it was done conveniently for them. They let me know, at the last minute, so I couldn't change anything.

I asked Kelly, 'How come you and Richard get interviewed, but I don't?' He told me that was the producer's idea. I said 'Come on, Kelly, I know you! You pull all the strings and call all the shots.' But he stuck to his guns and told me to speak to the producer, Danny O' Connor. But Danny told me they didn't have enough time to film me.

I asked him 'If I come down to London tomorrow, are you saying that you won't have the time to put a camera in front of me?' And he just repeated that it couldn't be done! But that was rubbish. He kept trying to explain, but in the end, I just put the phone down on him. At the end of the day – that's what every Stereophonics fan wants answered. Why didn't Stuart Cable get to give his opinion? Kelly thinks everyone walks around with their eyes blinkered. We all know that the people in charge get to rewrite history. When I was sacked Kelly and Richard posted something on the official website. When I wanted to put my side on there, the legal people at V2 Records said I couldn't do it.

So I told them that they should have stopped the other two band members as well. So really, I just sat there and thought this is going to be a farce – a joke – from start to finish, and it was. It cost Kelly and Richard a lot more money in the end. If they'd let me walk, it would have cost them peanuts. But they didn't and it cost them a fortune! Silly, silly people.

Stuart got a hefty pay-off from the band and he still gets royalties to this day from the back catalogue. Whilst he's recently, briefly, bumped into Kelly, I ask him if Richard has been in touch with him since the sacking.

No way. I haven't spoken to Richard since September 19, the day I left LA to fly home in 2003. I haven't got a lot of time for the gentleman to be honest with you. I bumped into Kelly at The Tragically Hip show in London and he had the audacity and cheek to say 'Richard misses you!'

So I told Kelly that my phone number hadn't changed and my e-mail address hadn't changed. He's missing me? He hasn't spoken to me in four years! Absolutely bizarre. Richard did admit in some interview he did in the *Swansea Post* newspaper that he hasn't spoken to me in four years. He didn't go into detail, but at the end of the day, Richard will toe the line for Kelly. Lots of people say to me 'You've got to realize that you got sacked from the biggest band in the UK. Some people might have slit their wrists, or put a noose around their neck. But you just got on with it. They are right! I just picked myself up, dusted myself off and set about getting on with it. I went into the TV work. I did the radio shows as well. Now I'm working for Kerrang radio and Xfm. I've got the new band happening. We're about to get a new record deal and record our first album. What a turnaround.

I wonder how long it took Stuart after the Stereophonics to get back into music.

Well, I was down. I'd be a total liar to say I wasn't. It was strange, because I'd had a call off the tour manager asking me where I wanted my drums sent to.

He laughs. I tell Stuart that it must have felt a bit like clearing your desk at the office.

Yeah. It was a little. But I spoke to John Brand. He asked me what I was going to do. I told him that I was probably going to take twelve months off just to chill out and do a few different things. I even told him I was considering knocking drums on the head and going into television full-time. John agreed I should take a break, but told me not to stop playing drums. He said I should start thinking about putting a band together. I spoke to friends and family and thought I'd give it a go. So John and I ran some adverts in *Kerrang* magazine for some musicians. But that was very unsuccessful. That was terrible, actually. It just didn't work out. So I started to think that maybe I couldn't have both the television work and the band. Look, I've played some of the biggest shows in the world. I've headlined the Glastonbury festival, the Reading festival, T in the Park, The V festival. I've played with Aerosmith, The Who, Bon Jovi, the Stones, U2 – done all these amazing things. I thought that was pretty cool, but I was starting to wonder if it was over, and maybe I should stick to the broadcasting.

Then, strangely enough, the whole Killing For Company thing took off. I'd started playing again, and met the right musicians, and it fell together – as it should really.

Despite the bitter way his time with the band ended, he still looks back with immense satisfaction and pride at his time with the Stereophonics.

What am I most proud of? Well, there are many defining moments. Playing in front of 50,000 people at the Morfa stadium in Swansea is one. Morfa was huge. Cardiff Castle was cool, because we were the first band there since Queen and then the Stones played there. Selling two million records of *Performance and Cocktails*. All the awards we won, which were voted for by the people who cared for the band. They were pretty special. The loyalty of the fans was incredible. They stuck by the band and spent a lot of money, time and effort to come to the gigs and buy our records. So all those things were great. There are far more wonderful memories than bad memories, by a long way. The places we toured were out of this world. To think that three kids from a mining village in the back end of nowhere, called Cwmaman, could do all that! I mean it's a cool place, but you don't think you're going to rise to stardom – and in such a short time. It's a shame the way it ended, but I've had a blast, man!

The Stereophonics chapter of his life is now over. But Stuart is driven by his love of music. The new band, Killing For Company, has got him purring again. They're heading for success. For Stuart, lightning could very well strike twice. His new group are thriving. I saw them take to the stage to support The Who. Mingling backstage, Killing For Company were getting a taste of the big time. It's a heady brew that the former Stereophonics drummer has enjoyed once before.

10

KILLING FOR COMPANY

Now I'm branded the evil one. I've split two bands up.
                                            Stuart Cable, Cardiff, 2007

It's a sunny April day as I watch Stuart Cable pull up outside The Beverley pub in Cardiff. He parks the huge black Range Rover and steps out. He's wearing a black West Coast Chopper biker T-shirt, white cowboy hat and jeans. Stuart has just finished recording in Monnow Valley Studios in Monmouth. His new band, Killing For Company, has laid down six tracks for a demo CD with Manic Street Preachers producer Greg Havers.

We take a seat inside the pub and Stuart tells me how he started this new band. It's a process he's taken his time with to make sure he's got the right musicians.

> It all started through a mutual friend, really, my former drum tech Swampy, as we call him, or Chris Stone. When I left the Stereophonics, we stayed friends and he said to me one day as we were sitting and having a pint, 'I know just the guitar player for you. I was in college with him. He's called Andy Williams and he plays in a band called The Sheer Shock Revival.' So I asked for Andy's number, called him and he came up for a jam and a chat.

So Andy Williams travelled up to Aberdare to play with Stuart. And the drummer was impressed by the wiry figure cranking out the riffs in front of him.

> When I first met up with Andrew in the rehearsal room, it was amazing. The only way I can describe Andrew is that he looks the way a guitar player should look. In the same way that Jimi Hendrix put a guitar on, and you can see straight away that his hands were built for playing guitar, well, it's the same with Andrew. As soon as he put the guitar on, I knew he was the right one for the band.

Andy then told Stuart about his brother Steve, who also played in the highly rated The Sheer Shock Revival. Steve was the bassist and lead vocalist. He joined his brother and Stuart for the next rehearsal.

> The three of us had a jam and it worked really, really well. So for a long time – about eight months – it was just Steve, Andrew and myself. Steve was doing the vocals at the time. But no disrespect to Steve – I like his voice – but I don't think it was quite right for us. We needed something with a bit more balls in it, really. So I asked Steve if he could just play bass, while we looked for a lead vocalist. And Steve was cool with that.

Now came the hard part – finding the right frontman for this emerging group. Stuart puts his drink down on the table, holds his head in his hands and groans as he remembers the process.

> We had this audition. About twenty singers came down for it. But it was awful. Just terrible! Some of the worst singers I've ever seen in my life were there. Not just from Wales, but from across the whole country.

So, end of round one, and Stuart was floored. Knocked out. The audition was a wash-out. But he was about to be touched by Lady Luck. Stuart was working for BBC Wales television on a new 'battle of the bands' style show. It was here that he'd stumble across the right man for Killing For Company.

> I was doing this thing for the BBC, which was basically looking for the next big band. We started off in north Wales and worked our way down south. And the last one we did was in in my home town, Cwmaman. It was in the little theatre, near where I was born and bred. It has a nice big stage with about 300 seats. This band from Cardiff called The Teeth came on. All I could see was their singer running around the stage like an idiot. He was all over the place. He was so captivating to watch. And best of all, he had a great voice. I thought 'He's the man I want!'

So Greg Jones joined the band at rehearsals and fitted in perfectly.

> I just can't believe how fortunate we've been. I can't believe just how well Greg and Steve's voices work together. They just fit together so harmonically. That's probably a million to one chance.

The four of them rehearsed and wrote songs together for about four months. Then they brought in a fifth member. Stuart wanted an extra guitarist, a rhythm guitarist to expand the band's sound.

Killing for Company

Killing For Company was filmed playing a 'mock' concert at The Point in Cardiff for the 2008 MacKenzie Crook film *Abraham's Point*. Hundreds of fans turned out on the day to be extras in the movie.

Singer Greg Jones was given lines to deliver in an eastern European accent. The lines read: 'Zdravo. Hello everybody. We have travelled a long way to be here tonight. So remember what is important in life . . . if you are not sure, maybe our first song will help! It's called "Zgradbi bika za jaja!" or "Grab the Bull by the Balls"!'

Well, Greg, fair play to him, said to me 'I didn't want to mention this before, but why don't we try Richie King from my old band, The Teeth?' Well that was fine by me, because Richie is a wonderful guitar player and exactly what we needed. I've always wanted to take this as far away from the Stereophonics as I could. Now, I'm a big lover of AC/DC, their guitars and the wall of noise that they can create. I've always wanted to have that big, big sound. So we were after another guitar player. We tried a few, but nothing worked out until Richie. He's our unsung hero. His guitar lines keeps our sound together. He's the backbone of the band. Richie is one of those guys who is a different kind of guitar player. He's like AC/DC's Malcolm Young, that essential second guitarist. You take his guitar line away and you really miss it.

But having recruited Andy and Steve from The Sheer Shock Revival and Greg and Richie from The Teeth, Stuart had poached talent from two Welsh bands with devastating effect.

'Now I'm branded the evil one. I've split two bands up.' Stuart laughs and shakes his head in disbelief. He's rarely been cast as the bad guy before and he's quick to explain that the situation isn't really as callous as it looks.

It needn't have been this way, as Killing For Company will take a while to get off the ground. It'll be a slow process. I was actually quite happy for the guys to carry on with their other bands, while we got this project off the ground. I tried to make it as friendly as possible, but it was the other members of the bands that threw their toys out of the pram. I told Rich to carry on gigging with The Teeth and he did – I saw three or four of their shows. I saw The Sheer Shock Revival play, and got on really well with them. But, all of a sudden, Andy, Steve, Greg and Richie could see that this thing was better than what they, were then doing. They knew from the sounds we were creating that this was something so special that it doesn't come together that often.

Stuart can now see the way ahead. After ten months' work, he's finally assembled a group of extremely talented musicians ready to hit the road and record.

I'm so blessed. This is very similar to the beginning of the Stereophonics. It's all about getting out there and giving people the chance to hear us. I know we can win over the crowds, wherever we go.

Stuart has that glint in his eye again. Despite his amiable persona and the jolly wisecracking, Stuart is a real leader. You sense he knows what he wants and how to get it. When it comes to his music, there is no messing about. This is no joke for him. It's a very serious business. With the line-up for Killing For Company settled, Stuart exudes confidence.

I know Greg is captivating. He's a very special frontman. I wanted a singer who could talk to the crowd, who's funny and quickwitted. And Greg is all that. He gets down into the crowd and sings and dances with them. He knows how to get the crowd going. When our old Stereophonics manager, John Brand, first saw us he said to me, 'I must apologize to you, Stuart, because for the first time in eleven years, I didn't watch you up on stage. I couldn't take my eyes off Greg. He's so captivating.' And that's exactly what I wanted.

We went into the studio at Monnow Valley about a month ago with about ten songs. We recorded six and now everyone's raving about our demo.

Stuart's also had some big news in the past twenty-four hours. He's heard that The Who have asked for Killing For Company to support them at their gig in July at Swansea's Liberty Stadium. I ask Stuart how this prestigious gig came about. He chuckles.

From me phoning The Who's singer Roger Daltrey! I know Roger from my days with the Stereophonics and the Teenage Cancer Trust gigs, which we always did with him. He's a really cool guy. When I got sacked from the Stereophonics, he rang me and said how appalled and disgusted he was about the way things were handled. He thought the band should have worked out its problems internally. He's very old school in that respect. He then told me that if I ever needed any help, I should just ring. So I remember someone saying I should call Roger and ask him about playing with The Who at Swansea. In the back of my mind I was thinking he'd answer the phone and say 'Stuart who?' But I plucked up enough courage.

76

It only took me about two days! Eventually I rang him and his wife answered the phone. I introduced myself, and she said Roger was away on tour, but gave me his e-mail address saying that it was the best way to contact him on the road. So I put an e-mail together and attached one of Killing For Company's songs: 'Say About Me'. I sent the e-mail, but after five days, I still hadn't had a reply. So I thought, 'Well, he's just deleted it! Never mind!' But then came a bizarre series of events. I had a phone call from a mate of mine in Swansea, who was wondering how he could get a box for The Who gig, as it was his fiftieth birthday on 1 June. So I thought 'The only person I know at the Liberty Stadium is the former Welsh rugby international, Scott Gibbs, who is a director for the Stadium's sponsors, Liberty Properties.' So I called Scott straight away. He was in the pub and said 'Yeah, we can sort that out.' Scott told me that the stadium was promoting The Who gig themselves. So he phoned this guy, Andrew Davies, who looks after the stadium. We had a meeting, and Andrew was happy to have us on the bill, though he said he'd have to confirm it with The Who. But, when he rang the band's management, they said they had already added us! At Roger Daltrey's request! And later when I got home, there was an e-mail from Roger saying 'I really like the song. Great to hear you're back. It's a band decision – but I did my best to get you on the bill.'

So hats off to Roger!

The Who gig will take Stuart full circle. His first big gig with Killing For Company will be with The Who. Ten years earlier, Stuart's first big gig with the Stereophonics was with . . . The Who!

'It's bizarre,' says Stuart, 'because one of the first major bands the Stereophonics supported was The Who in 1997 at Earl's Court on the *Tommy* Tour. Roger had really liked our first album. At the time, we were in Edinburgh with Kenickie. Do you remember them?' he asks me.

I do indeed remember them. Kenickie were a four-piece indie band from Sunderland. The band were named after their favourite character in the film *Grease*. They had a hit single in 1997 with 'In Your Car' before disbanding a year later after their second album. Their singer, Lauren Laverne, went on to be a TV and radio presenter.

'I love Lauren Laverne,' continues Stuart.

She's great. I did an interview with her a couple of weeks back, and I said something about Kenickie and she said 'Oh. We don't mention those days!!' So, yeah, we left that tour to go to play with The Who. So it's gone full circle. The first big gig for Killing For Company will also be with The Who. We're hoping to get back into the studio soon and do some new songs as well. But of the six we've already done, we're going to release one of those as a 'download only' release at the time of The Who gig. That's the plan. Let's hope it can chart.

Stuart and I order some food and more drinks. The Who gig is in less than three months' time. The band will spend that time rehearsing and playing a headline gig at The Point in Cardiff at the end of May as a warm-up for the main event just four days later.

28 MAY 2007 – THE POINT, CARDIFF BAY

When the time comes, The Point gig is a big success. Despite only having played a handful of gigs, Killing For Company are sounding sharp. Greg Jones, in particular, is revelling in his role as lead singer. Two songs in, and he's urging the crowd forward to fill the empty spaces at the front of the stage.

'You can all come a lot closer,' teases Greg. 'Come on. Someone's farted at the back. Let's get forward.' The band then launch into the terrific new song 'The Boy Who Saw Everything'. On this performance, they are ready for the big stage: the 22,000-capacity Liberty Stadium in Swansea.

Once the Cardiff concert is over, the band is beaming backstage. Amid much backslapping and hugging, the backstage area is awash with well-wishers, friends and relatives. All agree that tonight has been a resounding success. Big things are predicted. Stuart, in particular, looks pleased as he changes out of his stage gear.

I thought it went really well, actually. As a gig, I thought it was fantastic. This is the start of something big!

Can lightning strike twice? Stuart certainly thinks so. And by the smiles on the faces of his bandmates, so do they. But, first, a big test lies ahead. After just a few months together and only a handful of gigs, can they cope with the pressure of a high-profile performance on home soil?

11

WHO ARE YOU?

Where do I put this is? Well, it is still early days, but this is a big mile-stone. We're going to be the first band ever to play the Liberty Stadium and we're on first. Plus, we're supporting The Who. Need I say anymore?

Stuart Cable, June 2007

12 p.m., FRIDAY 1 JUNE

The big day has arrived for Killing For Company. It's the big gig! I arrive at Liberty Stadium with my friend and photographer Andrew Pritchard in tow. After being stopped by a succession of stewards at the front of the ground, we're instructed to drive around to the band area at the side entrance.

We park up, alongside a vast array of buses and trucks. A group of roadies carrying huge flight cases, covered in The Who logos, head into the backstage area.

Andrew and I explain to the security man at the gate that we are with Killing For Company. He finds our names on the guest list and points us towards the corner of the north stand.

I'd first been to this impressive new stadium two years earlier, just after it opened. I'd filmed a report for BBC Wales sport, having been given a behind-the-scenes tour of the stadium and all of its state-of-the-art facilities. A week later, I returned to report on the opening game at the ground, when Swansea City played a friendly match against Premiership Fulham, managed by one of their former players Chris Coleman. The match ended in a one-all draw.

The all-seater stadium has a capacity of just over 22,000 and is home to both Swansea City football club and the region's Ospreys rugby team. During its construction, a variety of names were suggested for it. At first the name Morfa was favoured, after a former athletics stadium on the opposite bank of the river Tawe. Next, the name White Rock was suggested after the copper works of the same name, which historically existed on the site. While a sponsor was being sought for the stadium, it was simply dubbed the New Stadium. But, eventually, after a sponsor-ship deal with Swansea-based developers Liberty Properties, it became the Liberty Stadium in October 2005.

Two years on from its opening and the venue is staging its first-ever concert. The 1960s icons, The Who, are visiting this £27 million venue as part of an European tour that kicked off in Lisbon two weeks previously. So far the tour has taken in Madrid, Bilbao, Birmingham, Sheffield and Newcastle, and will make its way across the continent until mid-July.

As Andrew and I walk towards the entrance into the arena between the north and west stands, we catch sight of Killing For Company bassist Steve Williams. The band had been in awesome form four days earlier at The Point in Cardiff – especially as it was only their fourth gig.

'Hi guys. Great to see you again. This is pretty fucking freaky, isn't it?' asks Steve, trying to light up a cigarette. 'I mean, The Who. This is so cool!'

Steve toured with the likes of Motörhead and the Stereophonics with one of his previous bands, Powder. But this is on another level altogether: a stadium gig with a legend of rock music.

'It's absolutely freaky!' agrees Andrew as we both shake hands with the bassist.

Steve takes us backstage. First stop is the canteen, which has been rigged up in an area behind the north stand. There are signs on every pillar on the way to the canteen, listing today's performance schedule:

Doors Open – 5 p.m.
Killing For Company – 6.15 p.m.–6.45 p.m.
The Charlatans – 7.15 p.m.–8 p.m.
The Who – 8.30 p.m.–10.30 p.m.

Inside the canteen, there are eight tables. Stuart Cable sits at the end of one table, wearing a straw cowboy hat with a red check lumberjack shirt and jeans. The table is full. The rest of Killing For Company are there – Richie, Greg and Andy plus members of the band The Last Republic, who are helping out as roadies for the day. We'd met them at the Cardiff gig a few days earlier. Guitarist Dafydd Anthony and singer John Owen are beaming like excited schoolchildren. They are thoroughly enjoying being part of this big occasion.

With his bandmates finishing up their meals, a hungry Steve Williams heads straight for the food. He's certainly not short on choice. The Who's travelling catering team has made sure that there is a vast array of food and snacks on offer. Each table in the canteen has a vase of flowers on it and there are plant pots everywhere. On the opposite side of the room to the food, there is a fridge full of soft drinks and a table with tea- and coffee-making facilities. The canteen is cordoned off by a thick black drape on three sides. Behind the main food stand, huge clouds of steam rise in big puffs as the cooks prepare the food for the bands.

Andrew has brought a present for each of the band members. He has selected close-up shots of all of Killing For Company, and the guys from The Last Republic, which he shot at The Point a few days ago, and is now handing them out. The musicians are delighted that Andrew has captured such good shots of them.

'Thanks, Andy,' says Stuart whacking him playfully on the back. 'That's a great souvenir of our first headline gig.' He peers closely at the big picture. 'Hey, I look pretty damn good, don't I guys?' and he flashes the photo at the band, who look vaguely in his direction. Greg waves a hand in a dismissive gesture and smiles. 'Yeah, you look great. In your dreams!'

Andy also has one for me, a shot of me on stage introducing the band. My big rock 'n' roll moment!

We leave the canteen area with Greg. Andrew and I give each other a smile and a knowing glance, as we walk out into the arena. Like The Last Republic guys, it does feel good being behind the scenes of such a big stadium gig. The buzz is infectious.

Out in the sunlight, the stadium looks so different to what I was used to on match day. But today, the grass is gone. The pitch has been removed and standing alone where the centre spot should be on the halfway line is a huge tent. It's the sound desk. But the tent suddenly looks tiny as we round the corner and see the vast stage area, towering over the empty arena.

The stage itself is at one end of the ground: the far end which, during the football matches hosted here, is usually occupied by the away fans. A massive grey canvas covers the stage. A team of twenty-five has spent the past four days constructing this gigantic stage. At the bottom right of the stage is a small flap. Well, it looks small from a distance given the cavernous size of the stage. But when you stand next to it, the entrance is actually more than eight feet tall.

A series of cases are being wheeled up a ramp and in through this side entrance and onto the stage. A dozen red flight-cases scored with The Who's logo sit just outside. Surrounding them are dozens and dozens of black flight-cases. A small folk-lift truck sits nearby waiting to help carry

---

Who Are You?

For The Who's 2007 European tour, their stage measured 50 metres high by 20 metres wide and weighed 150 tonnes. It took two 50-tonne cranes to help build the stage. To get it to the Liberty Stadium, the stage was transported across Europe on eight articulated lorries!

---

the gear to the stage area from the equipment trucks just outside the venue.

Overall, a huge crew of more than 250 people, including sound technicians, pyrotechnicians, security and roadies, are here putting the finishing touches in place ahead of tonight's extravaganza.

The stage itself features a gigantic video screen, which can be split into three parts during the show. There are two more huge screens – one on either side of the stage. Huge speaker systems are suspended from scaffolding on either side of the stage area. This is where music honed in the studio is brought to life.

Greg spies a lower platform in front of the stage. This is where the photographers will be during the gig. Greg smiles and claps his hands together in delight, like a small child who's discovered a gloriously muddy puddle to splash about in! 'Yes!' he exclaims in delight. 'I'll be nipping down to visit the photographers during the set. Oh yes!' When performing, Greg loves to clamber all over the stage, climbing monitors and speakers, or jumping off stage to clamber over tables, alcoves and the like. He's the singing equivalent of an extreme sportsman. He mixes singing with gravity-defying feats of climbing and jumping. Later tonight, he'll leap off The Who's stage to wander among the photographers as he sings, while his colleagues play their hearts out above him.

Eventually, we leave the stage area and follow Greg into the lifts on the ground floor. The artists' dressing rooms are all up on the third floor in the stadium's hospitality suites. These have been converted to dressing rooms for the day.

Once there, we see that room number 21 is Killing For Company's. Next door is number 23. This is home for the day to The Charlatans: the other support act on the bill.

Further down the corridor, The Who have taken over seven rooms on this floor. There is one for accounts, one for wardrobe, a big office for the production guys, two lounges for The Who's backing band and one suite each for the main men: Roger Daltrey and Pete Townshend. They occupy rooms 28 and 29, while their band are in 26 and 27. Filling out The Who's sound is keyboardist John Bundrick, bassist Pino Palladino, drummer Zak Starkey (son of Ringo) and guitarist Simon Townshend (brother of Pete).

The Who's dressing room area is full of flight cases. There are ten of them strewn across the corridor. These are not full of equipment, but clothes! One is open. Inside, a flamboyant white shirt is clearly visible at the front of an array of trousers and tops.

There's a security guard outside the lift making sure no stalkers, music journalists, fans or general undesirables get through to the bands. He asks for our VIP passes. Greg flashes his, but Andrew and I explain that ours are inside the band's dressing room. Greg vouches for us and, despite a very suspicious look, the guard waves us through provided we show him our passes as soon as we get them.

We move inside the Killing For Company dressing room. The band's suite is around ten foot wide by twenty foot long. By the door, there is a fridge is full of beers and soft drinks, and a bottle opener secured to the fridge with string! Clearly you can't trust such a motley bunch of rock stars. There's a TV on the back of the wall, which is showing the drama *Murder She Wrote*.

The front of the room has a set of sliding patio doors, which lead to the seating out front, overlooking the arena. Unfortunately, the view is of the side of the stage. So when watching The Who later this evening, the band will have to decamp to a special lounge down on the first floor. Andrew and I wander outside to watch the stage being set up. We peer to our left, across the seating, to see if The Who are here yet. But there is no sign of life in their dressing rooms.

Inside the room, sitting at a table, is the band's manager, Jo Hunt. She is busy sorting out the guest list and the VIP passes. There are family and friends to be catered for. For brothers Steve and Andy Williams, Swansea is their home town. They've had about 5,000 requests for tickets! Some will be disappointed. Actually, quite a few will be disappointed.

Andrew and I are given our VIP passes, and so the threat of being booted out of the stadium has gone. We breathe a sigh of relief. As I exchange greetings with the rest of the band, Andrew sets up his laptop and puts on a slide show of pictures from the band's last gig in Cardiff.

As the slideshow starts, Richie and Andy amble over, beer in hand, to study the shots from Monday's gig. 'I've got scary eyes,' says Richie watching three successive shots of himself on stage. 'God! Why is every shot of me is like this!' He pulls a manic face with eyes bulging wide. It's the classic serial killer pose. John from The Last Republic joins us. He catches a shot of Richie and jumps back in mock fright. The picture shows Richie poised with guitar pointed out at the audience like a machine gun. 'Fuck. He's gonna kill someone. Just look at him. Look at those evil eyes!!'

Stuart Cable laughs at that comment and eyes up Richie. 'Yeah,' he says. 'Definitely a serial killer. There's no doubt about that!' Richie opens his eyes wide in mock alarm. 'Ahh, come on guys. I don't look that bad.' He stares closer at the screen. 'Ok. Ok. Maybe I do.' He wanders off to find solace elsewhere.

Stuart is flitting in and out of the room. As the band's leader, he has things to arrange and people to see. He's also being interviewed by radio, TV and newspapers about tonight's gig. In between phone calls, I ask him if he's enjoying the build-up to this gig and, given the band's relative inexperience, how much he's looking forward to tonight.

'I'm hugely looking forward to it,' he tells me, suddenly looking very serious.

With the Stereophonics, we worked really hard and it paid off. It paid dividends. For example, at Cardiff Castle we played to 10,000 people. At the old Morfa Athletic Stadium here in Swansea, it was 50,000. Then later at Cardiff's Millennium stadium, it was a mind-blowing 70,000 people. But I know that with Killing For Company, we have to start at the beginning. I have to start again from scratch. That's cool though. I wanted to do this band. I wanted to put it together and I wanted everybody to have fun and that's what it is at the moment. It's great fun. Where do I put this? Well, it is still early days, but this is a big milestone. We're going to be the first band ever to play the Liberty Stadium ever and we're on first. Plus, we're supporting The Who. Need I say anymore? It'll be very interesting though. The crowd won't have heard any of our songs before on the radio, or anywhere. So we'll see if we can win them over. I bet we do!

And with a smile and a twinkle of the eye, Stuart's out of the door once more, this time for an interview with BBC Radio Wales.

It's now 2 o'clock. Tension is rising among the band members. They are getting restless, itching to get on with things. They are scheduled for a rehearsal at 3.30 p.m. But they have been warned that if things overrun during the soundcheck for The Who, that slot may have to be cancelled.

With the gates not yet open, outside the stadium floor is still deserted, save for a few of the stage crew. It's a very surreal sight, yet strangely beautiful in its emptiness. It's a gorgeous, sunny day, which brings out the best in the wonderful new stadium. With the pitch shipped out, the arena floor is lit up by the bright afternoon sun, giving it a stunning yellow haze. It resembles a vast desert. Like its very own oasis, the only thing visible in this vast expanse is the sound booth, which is covered by a sloping grey canvas. It looks like a nomadic tent pitched in this desolate wilderness for the night. Ironically, later on tonight, it'll be lost – surrounded by thousands of rock fans.

From our hospitality suite, I can see The Who's road crew scurrying over the stage like ants. One is shifting a keyboard into position. Nearby, two other crew members are putting the final touches to the main drum kit.

Turning to gaze down the other end of the stadium, away from the stage, I see two men working on a pair of giant spotlights. These lights are six foot long and resemble missile launchers. The two guys are working furiously to get them hooked up and operational. Cables are delicately put into place. Panels are opened on the side of the lights. And there is much fiddling and adjusting as the technicians try to find the right settings.

Back inside the dressing room, Stuart has returned. He's not in a good mood. The BBC interview did not go well. In fact it didn't go at all.

God, they kept me waiting for fifteen minutes in the heat, miles away in the blinking car park at their radio van. So I wait until they say the presenter in the studio is ready to talk to me – and that fifteen minutes seemed to last forever – then the reporter says they can't really do the interview now and could I come back in an hour. Well, what a nerve. I'm not here for their convenience. So I told her nicely that I had lots of work to do preparing for tonight, plus a soundcheck coming up and I couldn't come back. What a waste of time!

Stuart shrugs his shoulders, grabs another drink and takes a seat. In front of him, the two former members of The Sheer Shock Revival are pacing about nervously. For Steve and Andy Williams, this is by far the biggest gig they will have ever played. In 2000, in a band called Powder, they played at The Extreme World festival in Singleton Park in Swansea supporting Motörhead and Therapy! Andy says 'that was our biggest gig to date. And we got to meet Motörhead!'

'Yeah,' says Steve. 'That was great. Lemmy was a top guy. He was very accommodating when we were there. He didn't give me any of his Jack Daniels, though, the tight bastard!' Steve laughs. 'But then he shares that with no one.'

My friend Andrew stops taking photographs for a moment and looks at Steve with a big, broad smile. I feel some one-upmanship coming on.

'Well,' Andrew starts. 'That's not quite true.' He turns to look at me. 'Is it, Jeff?'

I stay quiet as Andrew retells the story of my interview with Lemmy a year earlier. The Motörhead singer insisted I drank a shot of his Jack Daniels after every other question during our interview.

'And he gave the finger while I took his photo with Jeff,' explains Andrew proudly.

Steve and Andy laugh. 'Good on you, Jeff. Drinking Lemmy's JD. Excellent result! We had our photo taken with the band though. One of my friends was carrying his mate's baby. He walks up to Lemmy and asks "You don't mind if we have a photo with the baby do you?" Lemmy looks at the baby, prods it gently and then says "Sure. No problem." So, we're all there with Lemmy having our photo taken. Lemmy's giving it the devil horns. It was wicked, man.' Everyone laughs.

'He has such a presence,' says Steve. 'Such a big guy, as well. So tall with his boots on. Wasn't he one of Jimi Hendrix's roadies?'

I reply that he was indeed one of the legendary guitar player's road crew, but he doesn't remember a lot about that period because of the drugs. 'I'll bet he doesn't,' laughs Steve.

We then discuss the merits of Lemmy's autobiography *White Line Fever*. Our conclusion is that it's almost as good as Mötley Crüe's astonishingly, and brutally, truthful book, *The Dirt*.

As we all sit down with a beer to try to chill out and relax ahead of the hoped-for soundcheck, Steve tells us about the band Powder. I knew they'd been hotly tipped to succeed and had won the Kerrang Magazine Unsigned Band of the Year Award. But little else apart from that.

Well, the Motörhead gig was the very next year after that award. So that was a great twelve months. But, eventually, we ran out of money. We'd signed with Mighty Atom Records in Swansea and helped set them up. The label eventually moved to a bigger studio. It was a wicked time. The band Funeral For A Friend joined around then as well. We spent our time gigging from Land's End to John O'Groats, but our bucks just ran out. It was going so well. It was only the poor finances that brought it to an end. But, hey, here we are now at The Who gig, so everything is for a reason I guess. If Powder hadn't split, then there'd have been no Sheer Shock Revival. If we hadn't been in that band, then we probably wouldn't have been asked to join Killing For Company. But now we're here, so it's worked out great.

Funnily enough, first of all – before Powder – I was in a band called Mother Nature and we supported the Stereophonics. That's how we first met Stuart. It was a great gig. We set up a big pyrotechnics display on the stage and didn't tell anyone. It was a giant confetti cannon. And Stuart, Kelly Jones and the boys were on the side of the stage watching us. Someone warned them: 'You should move back. They've got a pyro here.' The Stereophonics just told them to shut up. But it was huge like a bomb, when we set it off. It was so loud, I couldn't hear the first two songs we were playing. I was asking the other guys, 'Hey, what we playing boys?' This confetti cannon was so damn loud. And for the rest of the gig – even when the Stereophonics were on – there was all this paper still coming down. I don't think Kelly was very happy with that, but Stuart thought it was a real laugh. It's a mad small world! But we've only really become good friends with Stuart over the past two years, even though we've kind of known him for about ten years. I think that Stereophonics gig was about the same time that Stuart first met The Who – around about 1998.

He shuffles nervously in his chair and takes a massive swig of beer.

I'm looking forward to the soundcheck. It's gonna be great. Amazing. Me and Andy, as brothers, both come from Swansea and we're gonna be the first people to play this place. That's so cool. It's our home town. We're Swansea boys. [Richie's from Cardiff, while Greg's from Aberdare.] So the family will all be here. I'm not sure how many we have coming. Fifty, I think. Everyone's very excited.

There's a knock on the door and in walk The Charlatans. Stuart greets the band and then introduces his guitarist, Andy Williams. After a short greeting and a few exchanged jokes and smiles, The Charlatans return to their dressing room. 'Great lads,' says Stuart. 'I've met them before and we went out on the piss in Swansea. Great night that was!'

3.30 P.M.

Time is ticking away. There are now growing fears about the possibility of the soundcheck being cancelled. The Who's crew were supposed to have finished half an hour ago. But they've overrun, and are eating into the rehearsal time for the support bands. Stuart has been down to the stage and has seen the stage set-up. Killing For Company has to be squeezed in between The Who's gear and The Charlatans's equipment. Stuart's worried that Steve Williams's bass and monitor are too far away from his drum set. Stuart's drums are in the middle of the stage, while Steve is way out on the far right of the stage – quite a way from him.

This might make it difficult for Stuart to hear what Steve is playing and so could disrupt the smooth running of their rhythm section.

The band is still hoping they can get a rehearsal, but The Who's sound-check seems to still be going strong. Down on stage, the drums sound out a rapid beat, while every now and again the keyboards float gently over the top. Then both instruments stop sharply. After a pause, a high keyboard note rings out. Then the drums return for just a few seconds. The Who's sound guys are clearly still not happy. Killing For Company will just have to wait.

Steve stifles a yawn, leans back in his chair and sings 'Ho ho ho – It's rock 'n' roll!' while down on the stage a guy in a white beanie hat and black T-shirt now starts strumming away on an acoustic guitar. The waiting continues.

Killing For Company's sound guy Steve 'Hoppy' Hopkins comes in. 'What do you want in your monitors?' he asks the band.

'Everything,' says Andy quickly.

Steve Williams looks up and says 'Bass drum and snare please. That'll do me.'

Hoppy also has worries about the positioning of the bassist on stage. 'You'll be the other side of The Charlatans's drum kit. Well away from Stuart. It could be tricky.'

'In that case,' says the bassist, 'I definitely wouldn't mind a rehearsal, so I know what it sounds like. I want to know what to expect.'

The waiting continues. And continues. It's nearing 4 o'clock. The gates to the stadium open to the public in an hour. Despite the wait, the band are extremely excited. Every now and again, I catch them exchanging big grins and smiles. They also can't resist the odd high-five if passing each other. It's like watching a bunch of big kids as they wait for the jelly, ice cream and cake to be served at a party! They are also more than a little nervous. And with good reason. As a group, Killing For Company have only done four proper gigs.

The first one was at a benefit concert for Burberry workers, who were battling the closure of the clothing giant's factory in south Wales. The second was at a fireworks festival in Chepstow. 'A shambles,' Steve says. 'That shouldn't really count as a proper gig.' Then there was a charity show in Aberdare and, finally, last week's headline gig at The Point in Cardiff. On stage in Cardiff, the band were almost flawless. They played together as a tight unit – looking like they'd been touring together for months. The songs were outstanding and the audience loved it.

But tonight's different. I can't help but worry. Has this big gig come too early for Killing For Company? On the evidence of the Cardiff gig, they should pass this latest test with flying colours. But they do lack live experience on stage. And tonight the spotlight will shine very closely on them. Playing a huge stadium in support of one of rock's most legendary acts will be a huge challenge.

12

TESTING, TESTING! CAN YOU HEAR ME?

Oh my God! You just snubbed Scott Gibbs!
Killing For Company bassist Steve Williams, June 2007

4 P.M., 1 JUNE 2007, LIBERTY STADIUM, SWANSEA

The waiting for rehearsal drags on. 'It has to be near now,' I suggest optimistically to the band to try to ease their nerves. Going on stage without a soundcheck would not be good for their confidence on such a big occasion. While we wait, the conversation in the dressing room turns to television.

'I don't watch TV,' claims Andy Williams as we discuss a recent TV documentary about a reunion of the 1990s boy band East 17. The programme saw this short-lived reunion implode on the screen, as band members fell out and started fighting. It was pure car-crash TV!

The reason I don't watch the television is not for any great social theory, but for a very practical reason. I got really pissed off with what I was watching one night. So I picked the TV up and threw it out of the window. I looked down and it was in pieces outside. So I just use the Internet now. It's much more interesting. I must admit I think I've got a thing about TVs. In one house, where I used to live, we used an air rifle instead of the remote control. We would fire it at the channel buttons to turn over the TV stations. We did so much damage to the buttons that we only had BBC2 left at one stage!

4.10 P.M.

Finally, there's a knock on the door. 'Here we go boys,' says Stuart leaping up out of his chair to get the door. It's one of the stage hands. It's time. Killing For Company get their rehearsal slot on the big stage. So the band, along with Andrew and me, walks to the lifts and go down to the backstage area.

We walk slowly, almost *Reservoir Dogs* style (yeah, right!), up a steep ramp from the floor of the Liberty Stadium and into the huge opening in the side of the stage. From the dressing room, this looked like a small dot on the massive canopy that covers the huge stage. But now we're next to it, it's a cavernous opening. We pause and look through to the huge stage. Only Stuart has ever experienced anything on this scale before. And sure enough, he's first through, onto the stage, and starts setting up his drums. Once the main bit of his kit is in place, he gives a big stamp on the bass pedal. It booms and echoes around the empty arena. 'That fuckin' works,' he announces, proudly beaming from ear to ear. Next Stuart crouches down to attach the cymbals. Andrew nudges me. 'Look! Stuart's cymbals are all numbered so he knows where they go!' This strikes us both as very clever. But then again we're both so disorganized that such a simple show of practicality is bound to be impressive.

Stuart's cymbals are brought out one by one and he slots them into place according to number. Once the six drums are fitted together, Stuart sits behind them. At the same time, the two guys from The Last Republic are both scuttling around the stage at a furious pace, dragging bits of Killing For Company equipment, including amps and microphones, from the back of the stage to the front. John and Dafydd are in their element. At the previous gig in Cardiff, where their band supported Killing For Company, they volunteered to help today, more in hope than expectation. But their offer was accepted and now these budding musicians also find themselves on The Who's stage.

Stuart starts to bang out a fierce beat on his kit. 1–2–3–4. After this, it's decided that the front monitors need to be repositioned. They are dragged by Stuart and the crew members a little more over to the right-hand side of the stage. Stuart crosses the stage – spots me – and says 'Bloody hell! What a mad rush.' Obviously, the occasion can get to anyone. The big monitors, to the side of the band, are stacked one on top of the other. On their sides are wheels, so they can be easily tipped over and moved at the end of the show. More practicality in action! Stuart now greets his two guitarists, Andy and Richie, as they take centre stage and start strapping on their instruments. 'There's not much room for you guys,' he says, 'but we're trying to do the best with the space we have.'

Then Stuart turns to his bass player, 'Sorry, Steve, but you're over on the far side of the stage.'

I joke that it's not just the far side of the stage, but that Steve is actually way over on the other side of the stadium stand, and out in the car park.

'Yeah,' laughs Stuart, 'you're right over by the equipment trucks!'

Giggling to himself, a jovial Stuart returns to his drums. Sitting down, he taps the skins with a tuning key to test them, banging each skin gently to see if it is taut enough.

Greg Jones now shuffles onto the stage. The singer fiddles with his ear-piece until he's happy it's comfortable. Then he leaps down onto the lower platform, which has been set up to house the photographers. He'd promised to do this earlier.

'That's right,' shouts John, the adopted roadie. 'Greg's on the bass bins already!' Greg has leapt from the platform to The Who's big bass speakers. But getting back up to the stage proves more tricky.

In reference to the iconic headline act today, and with a straight face, I remind the band not to smash their guitars into The Who's expensive speakers, or kick the monitors off the stage at the end of their set. The band laugh. I hope I haven't given them any costly ideas! Dafydd now hands the setlist around, while John sticks copies to the floor of the stage by each of the front three microphones.

The setlist reads:

'She Won't Wait'
'Enemies'
'The Boy Who Saw Everything'
'For The Taking'
'Secret Lives of Empty Bottles'
'Even After All'
'Say About Me'.

The guy in the sound desk tells Stuart across the talkback system, 'Ok, we're ready to go. Kick drum, please.' Stuart does as instructed and the kick drum echoes wildly around the still empty stadium.

While Stuart goes through his paces, Greg is ambling around very relaxed. 'The show on Monday really helped me,' he says. 'That was a killer show. It's the longest set we've played yet and it rocked,' he says, referring to their warm-up headline gig in Cardiff. 'It settled my nerves, so I'm not so anxious about this gig any more. It's exciting. This is a buzz. Nerves of excitement, not fear, are kicking in! This is only the fifth gig we've ever done. It's mad. In fact, it's only my thirtieth show as a singer. So this is not bad for gig number thirty-one.'

Then Steve and Andy step up to the plate. Each takes it in turn to kick out a few licks and riffs, until the sound engineer says 'Thank you very much'. Then it's Richie's turn. After they are done, all three smile, unable to hide their excitement. Steve has a cool exterior. He's wearing dark sunglasses and has his hands in his pockets in a 'devil may care' stance. It's Andy, though, who looks the most nervous. Occasionally, he goes very quiet and looks quite pensive. Not your usual lead guitarist then! Richie is also quiet, standing at the front of the stage smiling. But it's clear that all three have throughly enjoyed the soundcheck and a chance to try out the impressive stage.

In the meantime, Greg is testing the microphones. He's singing, whooping and yelling. Finally, he sings the chorus to 'Say About Me': 'That's not what they would say about me.' Finally, the sound desk is happy, and as a bonus asks the band if they'd like to play a song. 'Too right, we would!' says Stuart. The band all nod in unison. They start up the opening to 'She Won't Wait'. Greg is off already. Even though it's only a rehearsal, he's down onto the speakers again. Me and Andrew are waiting in the wings, watching. To us, the band sound great, but Stuart is not happy. He can't hear the bass, only Andy's guitars.

'How can I keep time, if I can't hear the bass!' he shouts angrily across the stage. He's furious. This is an important gig. He doesn't want any technical problems to ruin the performance. Stuart wants the band to sound perfect. To do this, they have to be able to hear what each other is playing. One of The Who's technicians runs across to ask Stuart what he wants.

'I need to hear Steve's bass. Can we get it sorted?' The drummer is thoroughly annoyed. It's in moments like this that his professionalism shines through. It doesn't matter that The Who are the headliners and Killing For Company are just the support. His philosophy is 'If it's got to be done, do it well!' He absolutely will not put up with second best.

Judging Stuart's harsh tone of voice and his angry facial expression, the tech guy understands this straight away. He smiles, puts his hands up in the air in a neutral gesture and says 'No problem'. He then gives Stuart a thumbs-up before dashing back offstage.

'Can we run through the song again, or at least half of it?' asks Stuart.

'Well, no one's told me otherwise,' replies the guy at the sound desk. 'So you've got a few more minutes.'

So the band launch into the song one more time. When they finish, Stuart asks, 'Is everyone happy with that?'

Yes, they are. This soundcheck has been a success and has given the band a huge boost. 'We'll go with that,' says Stuart, as he thanks the stage guys. 'It's sounding good boys. Cheers.'

Steve Williams leaves the stage telling us how playing the soundcheck to an empty stadium reminded him of the Guns N' Roses video for 'Paradise City'. In that famous video, the song starts up while the stage is still being put together and the band are backstage. Then, they are seen rehearsing in front of an empty American stadium, before it gradually turns into the evening's live performance in front of a packed venue.

Back in the dressing room, the band has been visibly lifted by the experience of the soundcheck. It's all smiles and jokes now. The tension has all but gone. Now the wait to actually play is not a nervous one, but an exciting one. Stuart is off doing more TV and radio interviews. But he's left his mobile phone behind. It rings. Across the screen of the phone flashes the name of a famous Welsh rugby international. No one dares answer. When the phone stops ringing moments later, Steve points at Richie and jokes, 'Oh my God! You just snubbed Scott Gibbs!'

13

LET'S ROCK!
IT'S KILLING FOR COMPANY

I know we played a good gig, because my nipples are itchy. My nipples are always itchy after we play a good gig!
                                                Killing For Company guitarist, Andy Williams

5 P.M., THE DRESSING ROOM, LIBERTY STADIUM, SWANSEA

Stuart returns to the dressing room. He's in very high spirits, but he has a few nagging concerns, which he hopes won't affect their performance tonight.

He explains to me what some of the problems were during the rehearsal. 'I really need to hear vocals and bass to keep time. The guitars are obsolete to be honest – sorry Andy, boy!' He laughs as the guitarist flings his hands in the air in mock annoyance. 'No, seriously, if I've got the bass and vocals, then everyone's happy as we can all keep time. But Steve and his bass are so far away that it was difficult to hear him. That makes things hard.'

The band's manager Jo walks into the room and proudly announces that the band will have their new logo projected onto The Who's gigantic video screen during the show.

'While you were rehearsing, I sweet-talked the video projection guy,' she says.

'I don't want to know how!' quips Steve. 'Keep the details to yourself.'

'That's cool, Jo. Well done,' Stuart compliments his manager. 'That's going to look great – our name blazing out on The Who's big video screen.'

Then Stuart spies a very, very large pair of drumsticks on the table.

'Whose drumsticks are these?' he asks.

'I don't know, but they were in your bag,' says Jo, looking at the drummer quizzically.

'Oh my God! I'd totally forgot I'd brought these. They are my Cozy Powell drumsticks! I bought them after he died. I tried to get his drum kit, but got four pairs of sticks instead. Aren't they huge?! These are gigantic,' he says, spinning the unwieldy sticks in the air. 'How the hell did he not break his drum skins when using these?'

We wait, and wait, for the knock on the door that says 'showtime'. The gates have been open for an hour now and the crowd has slowly filtered in. One of The Who's management said they would come and get the band at 6 p.m. on the dot. It's now 6.05 p.m. and the band is getting twitchy.

'Should we go down anyway?' asks Richie.

'No way. They said wait. So we'd better. We don't want to piss off The Who!' chuckles Stuart.

A minute later and the big moment finally arrives. There's a knock on the door and the band is escorted down into the lift, and then taken backstage. We're led, once again, up the huge ramp and onto the left-hand side of the stage.

As soon as we get to the entrance, leading onto the stage, I notice how full the arena has suddenly become. After performing in an empty venue during rehearsal, around 9,000 fans have now entered the place. Most have taken up position in front of the stage.

The Who's stage manager greets the band and he has a question for them. 'As you are the first band ever to play this stadium, would you like someone to introduce you?'

The band glances nervously at each other and, after a few shrugs, all eyes turn to me. 'Jeff will do it!' announces Stuart confidently. 'Yeah,' says Steve heartily. 'He introduced us at The Point. He's getting good at this. Go on Jeff!'

Having been volunteered, I have no choice. I walk slowly out onto the vast stage – in front of me thousands of people must wonder what on earth is going on. Who is this strange person ambling to the front of the stage?

'Go on Jeff,' shouts a smiling Stuart from the back of the stage, while Steve simply gives me a thumbs-up sign. My mind suddenly flashes to thoughts of gladiators at the arena awaiting the arrival of the lions.

I look back at The Who's stage manager. 'Middle mic?' I ask. He nods in confirmation.

'Welcome to the Liberty Stadium!' I announce to the expectant crowd. They laugh. Sadly, I'd made a little error. Call it nerves. Call it stupidity. What I actually said, without realising, was 'Welcome to the Millennium

Stadium,' which is the national stadium of Wales, just down the road in Cardiff. Cardiff and Swansea are big rivals. But instead of being chased out of the ground, hung, drawn and quartered, the crowd laugh, assuming that I'm giving this venue the importance of the Millennium Stadium. They think it's a deliberate joke.

'We've a great evening ahead featuring the legendary Who,' I continue, unaware of my gaffe. 'But now the first band to play this wonderful venue [I think I redeemed myself here!] Get ready to rock. It's Killing For Company.'

Time to exit, stage left. The band walks on as I retreat to the wings to watch the gig from the side of the stage, surrounded by The Who's guitars and equipment. Killing For Company launch straight into 'She Won't Wait'. At the end of the song, Greg introduces Stuart and the crowd go wild, clap and chant Stuart's name. The drummer stands and takes the applause.

Andy on guitar is now all smiles. He had been the most nervous pre-gig. But he's revelling in this. Greg, meanwhile, is full of energy. He's the stereotypical coiled spring. He's very hyperactive and it's like watching a caged tiger as he paces restlessly across the stage.

Sure enough the band's logo is projected in massive letters above them on the gigantic screen. They're getting a fantastic reception.

'Come closer,' urges Greg to the few at the back of the stadium. The singer is rapidly winning over the crowd. By the second song, the crowd are clapping along, even though this is material they have never heard before.

Greg struts and swings the microphone wildly, looking like a cross between a young Roger Daltrey and Peter Gabriel. At the end of the song, Stuart throws his sticks into the crowd, who have been well and truly won over.

For the third song, 'The Boy Who', Greg has leapt down to join the photographers and has clambered up on the big bass speakers down at the front of the stage. He stays there for the next song as well, urging the crowd to sing. 'The Boy Who' is as near as dammit the perfect rock song. Steve Williams's seventy-mile-an-hour bass riff is eventually joined by Andy Williams and Richie King's clanging guitar chords as Greg Jones sings one of the catchiest verses – followed by a real sing-along chorus. By the end of this song it was game over. The band had successfully wowed another set of music followers.

'For The Taking' sees the band continue in top form, the stylish play-ing of lead guitarist Andy Williams impressing all, while Greg Jones in particular visibly growing in confidence and stature with every song. Whether stalking the stage, or clambering across the front of the speakers, the singer makes use of every inch of the stage in captivating style. His banter in between songs gets longer as his confidence grows. His humour is as enthralling as his stage presence.

For the song 'Secret Lives of Empty Bottles', it was the turn of rhythm guitarist Richie King to step to the fore. His sparkling, chiming and hypnotic riff is the core of this song. It shimmers and shines as the rest of the band add layer by layer of melody to make this song the perfect future single.

Ironically, Richie's style bears more than a passing resemblance to that of Pete Townshend in the way he throws his guitar in violent strokes around his tall, thin frame, while striking poses that wouldn't have looked out of place on a 1970s Who tour.

Richie's playing is at the heart of this band – the framework for the breakneck bass playing of Steve Williams, the delightful guitar sketches of Andy Williams and the frenetic and powerful drumming of Stuart Cable. Stuart's drumming is starting to resemble that of John Bonham. And I don't say that lightly. But, like the Zep legend, Stuart pounds his drums with a savagery and ferocity that looks like his life depends on hitting each note as hard as he can. He pounds the skins so hard, it's a surprise they don't break, or run for their lives screaming for mercy! He's enjoying the role of anchor in a hard rock band.

All too soon the band reach the final song 'Say About Me'. Greg sings the chorus to the audience and tells them they have to sing it back to him. When he's satisfied that the crowd knows the words and when to join in, Greg announces 'Bloody hell! They're better than me!' The song is the archetypal anthemic tune and a rousing way to finish the set.

Once off stage, the band is mightily pleased with their performance. 'That's our best gig yet!' beams Steve Williams proudly. 'I know we played a good gig, because my nipples are itchy,' declares Andy Williams. 'My nipples are always itchy after we play a good gig!' No one enquires further, but Andy's nipples are right. It was a very good gig. It's amazing to think this was only Killing For Company's fifth live performance.

After the show, Greg is delighted. Steve slaps hands with both me and Richie. 'Hey, Jeff! Do you know what?' he asks 'If we were the first band ever to play here, then your voice is the first voice ever to be heard at a concert here! That should be in Trivial Pursuit.' He smiles, grabs me and says 'Thanks for the intro, man. You're a star!' He pauses and then looks towards Andrew, Greg and Richie. 'But didn't we rock?' Greg laughs!

'Too right, we did!' Now Andy and Stuart stroll down the ramp towards us. 'What a buzz, man!' the drummer announces to his band. Stuart's hit the nail on the head. The whole band is buzzing. Everyone is smiling. It went well and the band knows it. We all head for the hospitality bar to get a well-earned drink and meet with up with friends and family.

Once in the bar, Richie meets up with his dad, who teases him about their resemblance. 'I don't look anything like you!' exclaims Richie. 'I don't think you look like your dad,' chips in my friend Andrew, camera still in hand. 'Cheers,' says Richie. 'You're a pal for life.' It's obviously these little things that are important and make life-long friendships!

'Nah,' says his dad, having none of it. 'You do look like me. And it'll get more so!' Richie groans, takes a big swig of beer and then, ignoring his dad's claims, reflects on the gig.

It sort of feels like any other gig. I try to take myself away from the fact that the size of the whole thing was so big. You're gonna do a show, but you walk out, see the size of the crowd and think 'bloody hell'. It's like a cramp at the top of your stomach that says there's no turning back. I'm here. That's it and I'm gonna do it to the best of my ability. After every song, the reaction from the crowd was amazing. I was raising my hand and giving a salute to the crowd. And seeing Greg doing his thing was amazing. It was big cheers after every song. I thought we sounded great and everyone in the crowd was clapping. When you start a new band, it normally takes a while to get it together, so to come in on the fifth gig to play a concert this size with such a legendary band is phenomenal. How many bands would give anything to be in this position and play with The Who? Now I've done it, I can't actually believe it's happened. I can't believe it's over and done. It felt like we were on stage for two minutes.

I leave Richie talking to his dad and Andrew. I stroll over to the bar where Stuart Cable is chatting to Jo and the band's press officer, Dave Clarke. I ask Stuart how he felt it went.

There's an old saying in Cwmaman and it goes 'What a week today's been!' And that's right, really. It was a bit of a nightmare, but it's been cool. It turned out kind of rosy and sunny. It was like going back to the early days of the Stereophonics. You've got to get on there and pinch people's fans. You've got to get people to your next gig. You've got to get people to buy your next record. I kind of like that in a strange way. It's a very difficult thing to do, because you've got to have the right kind of mental attitude and the right kind of get up and go. I've got to take my hat off to Greg. I think we've found ourselves a little star there.

Stuart spots Greg chatting away on the other side of the bar and raises his glass in salute at the singer.

The way Greg controls the crowd is amazing. If that's how he handles being the support, can you imagine what would happen if he was in front of an audience wholly here to see us. Just imagine how he'd handle that! He's everything I've ever seen, and wanted, in a lead vocalist. He has immense charisma. Everything he does is cool and he's so determined. He wanted people to sing that song tonight and he made them. He's got something. You're born with that kind of thing. He's got something that works.

I mention the crowd reaction. They loved Killing For Company. Stuart is pleased.

We're always aware of crowd reaction. I don't want to sound blasé, but I've been doing this a long time and I'm always gauging the crowd reaction. It's amazing to go full circle – back ten years – to the days of opening for bands and trying to win fans over onto your side. It's bizarre. Maybe I'm a bit too old, but I'm having fun. With the support slots, it's important to have fun. That's the main ingredient.

8.30 P.M., THE WHO TAKE TO THE STAGE

The stadium is now full. The Who take to the stage and launch straight into 'I Can't Explain', followed by 'The Seeker'. Pete Townshend is wearing a blue shirt, black trousers and shades, while Roger Daltrey is wearing a black T-shirt, black trousers and has on a pair of blue-tinted John Lennon- style glasses.

During the opener, 'I Can't Explain', the band suffer a power cut. The power fails on two more occasions during their fourth song, 'Who Are You'. During the first power cut, Pete Townshend grabs a can of coke from the top of a monitor and storms backstage.

'Apparently, we're too loud,' Townshend explains as the band eventually cut short the song due to the technical problems. Annoyed at not being able to end the song, Townshend says sarcastically, 'And for those who don't know how it finishes, it goes . . . 'Who are you. Who are you. Who. Who. Who are you' The audience roars with laughter at the guitarist's dry humour.

Watching the gig, Killing For Company's soundguy Steve 'Hoppy' Hopkins tells me, 'I haven't seen anything like this since the V97 festival.

Every time that The Prodigy tried to play "Smack My Bitch Up", they blew the left-hand side of the stage. I had to hold the breaker with my finger. You really do need a good generator.'

Song five from The Who is 'Behind Blue Eyes'. Beautifully played, there are no power cuts, prompting sarcasm from a disgruntled Who singer. 'A song from beginning to end. The wonders of modern technology,' quips Daltrey.

After a thundering 'Baba O'Riley', a twelve-minute version of 'My Generation', and 'Won't Get Fooled Again', Peter, Roger and band take their final bow. The first encore is 'The Kids are Alright'. The second is 'Pinball Wizard'. Despite the power glitches, the crowd have loved every moment of this gig.

Powerful search lights shoot from the stage into the sky, criss-crossing in the dark Swansea night as the rock legends prepare to sign off. During 'See Me, Feel Me', Stuart Cable plays air guitar, while watching Pete Townshend on stage and he finally punches the air in delight and appreciation of The Who's set. On stage, the song ends with Roger Daltrey spinning the microphone around over his head and Townshend's trademark windmill guitar – as it should.

The Who thank the Swansea crowd for coming on such a cold night. Daltrey has been singing the last couple of songs holding a cup of tea. He's also donned a jacket, which is firmly buttoned up against the chill night air. He signs off with 'Apologies for the breakdowns – shit happens – be lucky.'

Stuart taps me on the shoulder. 'I can't believe he said that! Kelly Jones told me that when he said goodbye to him many years ago, Roger said to him – in a cockney accent, "Be lucky, mate!" So for the next few weeks, all Kelly said to anyone was "Be lucky". You know, I didn't really believe him. But it's true.'

Killing For Company – like the rest of the stadium – has thoroughly enjoyed The Who's gig. They prepare for the after-show party. Are The Who going to join us? There are rumours that the rock legends are tired and will leave the stadium in the next few minutes. I've arranged to interview Roger Daltrey about his friendship with Stuart Cable. So Andrew and I dash out to the lifts and up to the dressing rooms. Andrew takes his camera out of its case as we wait with the stadium's security, while one of The Who's staff tracks down the singer.

As we wait, the security guard tells us that The Charlatans rarely left their room just opposite us, ordering in bottles and bottles of champagne. Finally down the far end of the corridor, we see Roger Daltrey, with a huge grey blanket draped over his shoulders. He beckons us down to his dressing room.

Inside it is a lot plusher than the room Killing For Company have been given. Two very comfortable sofas have been placed down one end by the patio doors. A big pot plant to one side adds to the feel of a cosy living room. I sit down next to Roger, while Andrew asks if it's OK to take a few pictures of the interview. Roger Daltrey is pleasantness personified. He asks if we'd like a drink, are we comfortable and chats generally about whether we've enjoyed the day.

But The Who singer is also clearly upset by the technical problems the band encountered during their show. He tells me he didn't feel the night went well. I try to reassure him by telling him that the crowd loved it and didn't mind the slight hitches, which were humorously dealt with by the band. He appears slightly reassured but, nevertheless, clearly a perfection-ist, he's still not happy about the power failures, which dogged the first four songs.

We're interrupted by a knock on the door and The Who's bass player, Pino Palladino, comes in. Pino was born in Cardiff, like Andrew and myself. He's played with some of the best musicians in the world, including Eric Clapton, Elton John and David Gilmour. He'd like to introduce his parents to Roger. The Who's singer turns to me to ask if this is ok and asks if I mind delaying the interview while he meets Pino's folks. This is no problem and we agree there are more important things in life than post- gig interviews. After the meeting, Andrew offers to take a photo of them all, an offer the family gratefully accept. The bassist and his family depart happy, following a good gig in Pino's homeland, and they will also have a lovely picture of the family gathering as a souvenir.

When Roger returns and again takes a seat next to me, I ask him why he chose the Stereophonics to support The Who way back in 1997.

'Wow,' he says with a smile. 'It's so long ago. My memory's getting foggy.' He sips his tea and laughs.

No, seriously, we always try to look for bands that we like and think might have a chance of making it. It's such a good spot supporting a band like The Who. And with the Stereophonics we were right. They were a great band. There was no pretence about them. They were what they were. And Kelly Jones had such a great voice. He never holds back. When he goes for it, he really goes for it. Even if he's feeling a bit rough, he never holds back and that's what a singer should do.

And as for Stuart, well, he's a great guy. He's helped me with the Teenage Cancer Trust. He's been very supportive with that and helped me with the shows at the Albert Hall. I've met them and they are friends of mine.

Roger caught a bit of the Killing For Company show and was impressed.

I loved the new material, which Stuart sent me. The songs were great. They are a tight band. I'd love to hear more of them. In this dressing room, I was listening to them and they sounded good – even though we're just behind the stage, so the sound wasn't perfect. But on record, they are a very strong unit with good melodies. I wish Stuart's band luck. I hope they enjoy what they're doing and can make a living out of it.

But, it's a bloody hard way to make a living in music, I'll tell you that. Even at our level, it's a lot of work. It's twelve-hour days, and a lot of sweat and travel. It's not easy. But good luck to them.

Having been told that The Who wanted to leave soon, I cut the interview short. But Roger is in a chatty mood. He's very amiable and we talk for another ten minutes about the state of the music industry, music shows on TV, the current state of UK radio and much more. I get the impression Roger would happily sit with us for another hour or so. As we leave his dressing room, both Andrew and I agree that he is one of the most pleasant rock stars we have ever come across.

Back in the Killing For Company hospitality area, the band are preparing to leave. It's been a very long and very exciting day.

For Stuart Cable, this day has seen his career come full circle. In 1997, his emerging band the Stereophonics were 'spotted' by The Who. Impressed by the Welsh trio, they were given a prestigious support slot on the band's *Tommy* tour. Now, ten years on, Stuart's new band also landed a big gig with The Who. Just the boost they needed. As everyone leaves the stadium, the verdict from band, family, friends and new-found fans is that this is the start of something big for Killing For Company.

14

ONWARDS AND UPWARDS!

The end of 2007, and start of 2008, was a good time for Stuart Cable and Killing For Company. 2007, though, concluded with a unexpected event. The Stereophonics were temporarily reunited at a friend's wedding. Stuart Cable, Kelly Jones and Richard Jones even played four songs on stage for the wedding guests. Past problems were put to one side for one night as the former friends chatted over a few drinks. It was the first time Stuart had played with the band since he left under acrimonious circumstances in 2003. But there was no animosity between the trio as they shared the stage at the wedding reception at the Cwrt Bleddyn hotel in Usk on 27 December.

The three had been invited to the wedding reception of Dave and Simone Roden from Ebbw Vale. Dave, a sound engineer, first met the Stereophonics twelve years earlier when he was hiring out PA systems across south Wales. He continued to work with them when they got signed to the V2 record label and helped them set up their sound system at some of the best-known festivals in Europe, including Glastonbury and Reading. He invited the three members of the original band to the reception separately and they all wanted to come and help him celebrate his big day.

Stuart told me that he'd accepted the wedding invite as Dave was such a good friend.

Dave Roden had been our front-of-house guy since before we had a record deal. He stayed with the band for a long time. He's such a lovely guy. He and his wife-to-be invited me. I wanted to go. And at the end of the day, this wasn't about me, Rich and Kelly. It was about him, his wife and their special day. He took the effort to invite me, so I figured I'd make the effort to go.

I hadn't planned to meet up with the other Stereophonics, but once there, I went to bar to get a drink. Kelly appeared behind me, asked how I was, and if I wanted a drink. Then, forty-five minutes later, he asked me to join him and his friends. So I went over to sit with them. Richard was there and also asked how I was. So we spent a while drinking and talking. It was nice.

Later, I went outside for a cigar and Richard came out as well. He asked if I wanted to play a song or two. I said we'd better ask Kelly. Kelly was up for it, so we did a few tunes in front of the guests.

We played 'Local Boy in a Photograph', 'More Life in a Tramp's Vest', 'Maybe Tomorrow' and 'I Wouldn't Believe Your Radio'.

But the night wasn't about us. It was about Dave. The three of us were civil to each other and we had a good night with no bad stuff from the past coming between us. We just focused on the future. I asked them about the Sterephonics and they asked me how things were coming along with Killing For Company. So it was a good night. A great laugh. We didn't even talk about the band after the performance. We just left it at that.

So the hatchet was buried for the evening. Maybe a few old wounds were healed, but the actions of the past aren't so easily forgotten. It's unlikely that the original Stereophonics will ever play on the same stage together again. That wedding reception witnessed a historic night!

Stuart's new loyalties lie elsewhere and by the end of 2007, Killing For Company were rapidly gathering momentum. The Who gig had been a landmark step for the band. They spent the next few months playing concerts across Wales to raise their profile locally. Then, a few months later they toured with US rock band, Tesla, which saw them playing at bigger venues across the UK.

The band would play two more landmark gigs. In March 2008, Killing For Company performed their first-ever acoustic set, when supporting the Alarm's frontman Mike Peters for a special gig at The Point in Cardiff for St David's Day. The band were nervous, but yet again rose to the occasion, eventually rejoining Mike Peters on stage for the finale: a rousing version of Neil Young's 'Rockin' in the Free World'.

A few months later, an outdoor gig at Cyfarthfa Castle in Merthyr Tydfil supporting Status Quo further cemented the band's live credentials, winning over yet more new fans with a typically energetic and anthemic display. By the summer of 2008, Killing For Company were ready to enter Monnow Valley Studios in Monmouth for a second time.

On 5 June, Andrew and I arrived at Monnow Valley Studios. It was 11 o'clock on a beautiful summer morning and the Old Mill House looked resplendent in white as we strolled up the path to the main entrance. As we walked we could hear the River Monnow flowing past, which is always a wonderful sound, and the scenery surrounding the studio is delightful to admire. It's no wonder bands love coming here to record. We're here to see Killing For Company as they record with producer Bob Marlette, who has flown in from Los Angeles especially to work with the band.

The time may be approaching midday but the band are still not up. The studio's owner Jo Hunt tells us that the band had a late night last night, drinking to celebrate the end of the long and tricky recording session.

The drinking session had ended at 4 a.m. with the band playing a practical joke on Stuart, who had passed out on the sofa in the main living room. Among others things, the band put cornflakes on their drummer's eyes, a replica guitar from the guitar hero video game in his hands and called up some dodgy porn on the nearby TV. Many other more unspeakable things were inflicted upon the unconscious body of the former Stereophonic. But photographs of how Stuart looked at the end of this prank have since been locked in a metal box, chained up and buried deep beneath a Welsh mountain for the sake of humanity!

As the clock ticks slowly past twelve, the band emerge slowly, one by one. Guitarist Andy Williams is first up. He's straight into the kitchen to make a cup of coffee. He's closely followed by producer Bob Marlette, while rhythm guitarist Richie King stumbles by with a bowl of Cheerios in his hand. Singer Greg Jones has also materialized and is far more perky as he breezes through the kitchen. Maybe he had a 'stunt double' to fill in for him last night as he seems unaffected by the lengthy drinking session. He bounds out of the kitchen, tea in hand and joins producer Bob Marlette out on the patio just outside the studio control room. This morning, the final day of the week's session, it's Greg's turn in the studio to lay down his vocals. 'Surrender' is the first song up and Bob coaches Greg on the vocal.

'How good's your range? How high can you go?' asks Bob. The two guitarists Andy and Richie are now both sitting around the patio table, under the huge sunshade, just opposite Bob and Greg. The producer asks one of them to play a chord: G. 'Lets see what you can do,' he challenges Greg. Greg sings the chorus to 'Surrender', which is one of the band's slower and more heartfelt songs. Bob shakes his head. He's sitting slouched in his chair, feet up on the table, acoustic guitar in his lap, wearing black jeans, black T-shirt and shades, with a huge cigar protruding from his heavily bearded face. His face barely moves, eyes still hidden behind the dark shades, as he tells Greg, 'I need more emotion! More yearning! I need to get you to a place where your head is going to explode!' As Greg tries again, his voice rises early. Bob cuts him short. 'Save it for the last line. That's the money line,' he enthuses. When Greg gets it right, after another three attempts, Bob pretends to be overly emotional. 'I'm crying with joy,' he says, 'it's why I'm wearing these sunglasses to hide the tears.'

Richie stares at him, causing the group to double up in laughter when he asks with a straight face, 'Do they call you "Blubbing Bob" back in Nebraska, then?'

Bob's CV reads like a Who's Who in rock: Alice Cooper, Black Sabbath, Ozzy Osbourne, Rob Halford, Glenn Hughes, Slayer, and many, many more. Bob Marlette tells a story about when he was in the band Quiet Riot in their early days in the late 1970s in LA.

We were always broke. We used to chat up the girls after gigs – I can't say they were groupies because no one knew who we were. But we'd be chatting up the cutest girls at the venue we'd just played because we needed a place to sleep for the night. We were that poor!

One night this girl I was talking to said I could stay at her place. She explained that it actually wasn't her place but her boss's. He was away for a month in Switzerland and she was house-sitting for him.

I turn up with my stuff hours later. She opens the door and lets me in and the first thing I notice on a shelf on the wall is a row of Ringo Starr bobble-heads! 'Wow', I thought, 'Her boss must be a big Beatles fan.'

Then as we walked into the main room, there was this amazing replica Beatles drum kit . . . a replica of the one they used on the Ed Sullivan show. It was the centrepiece of the room, which I noticed was also filled with a lot of Beatle's memorabilia. Seeing my stunned expression, the girl suddenly piped up, 'Oh yeah! I forgot to tell you. My boss is Ringo Starr!' So I spent three weeks crashing at the house of one of the Beatles. It was so cool. Later in the week, the doorbell rang. I opened it and there was George Harrison standing in front of me! 'Is Ringo there?' He said. I was so stunned, I simply said 'No, he's in Switzerland' and closed the door.

Bob also met Sir Paul McCartney in the US many years later. 'It was when the Beatles album *1* was top of the charts,' He recalls. 'I told him "Congratulations on yet another chart topper." "Yeah," replied Paul nonchalantly, "we did some quite good songs back then."'

While Greg rehearses some of the new arrangements that he and Bob have worked out, Stuart, Richie and Steve are in the studio's control room to hear a playback from some of yesterday's session. Stuart admits its was one of the hardest recording sessions he's ever had. 'Bob's such a perfectionist. He knows what he wants and he knows how to get the best from us. I've never been worked so hard. He wouldn't let me stop until it was absolutely spot on. And that's great. That's what I've always wanted from a producer.'

At the playback, Stuart and Richie are sitting on the sofa. Bob is in the 'big chair' in front the the mixing desk. To his left is a computer, and Bob taps a button and the band's song 'Even After All' booms out of the control room's speakers. Richie starts bopping along to the music. Stuart listens impassively, chin resting on his hand, while Steve is standing by the arm of the chair with a massive smile on his face. He looks at me and Andrew and says 'Hey! This really rocks!'

It's not Bob's first visit to Monnow Valley. He was first here with Black Sabbath guitarist Tony Iommi in the 1990s. He remembers that back then the sound in the control room was not that good. 'You would have to move your head around to hear the different sounds,' he says. 'I'd be shouting, "Where's the bass?" It's better now, though.' The new owners have removed all the old tiles above the desk and given the control room a thorough makeover so it sounds good.

Work finally begins at 2.30 that afternoon. Greg is locked in the studio with Bob, while the rest of the band are still recovering – in varying degrees – from the previous night's drinking session. 'I feel like I've got a Frenchman in my head,' moans Stuart, still stumbling slowly and carefully around the kitchen. But Stuart thoroughly enjoyed yesterday's drum recording session.

> I've been so keen to work with Bob Marlette. It's something I've always wanted to do: to work with a big name producer. And to get an opportunity to do so is great. It's been fascinating to get an outsider's eye on our material. He has plenty of ideas about how we can take things forward. That's wonderful.

The band learnt a lot from recording four tracks with Bob Marlette. They laid down 'Surrender', 'Even After All', 'Former Mining Town' and a reworking of 'Over'. It gave them more confidence in the studio and more ideas about what they could achieve.

A decade ago, Stuart was part of the Stereophonics, who rose to success at a time when record companies were loathe to look past London for new talent. Against all the odds, their talent and determination shone through. Despite being from a tiny, unfashionable village buried away in south Wales, they made the record companies sit up and and pay attention. In the time I've known Stuart, his affable, easy-going and joke-filled character is the first thing that you notice. But deep down, he is a dedicated musician. He wants to succeed. His drive and ambition have seen him rise to the top once before. Watching him in action with Killing For Company, it's easy to see his driving force propel his new band to greater heights. Lightning can strike twice.

INDEX